BY CHANCE A WINNER
The History of Lotteries

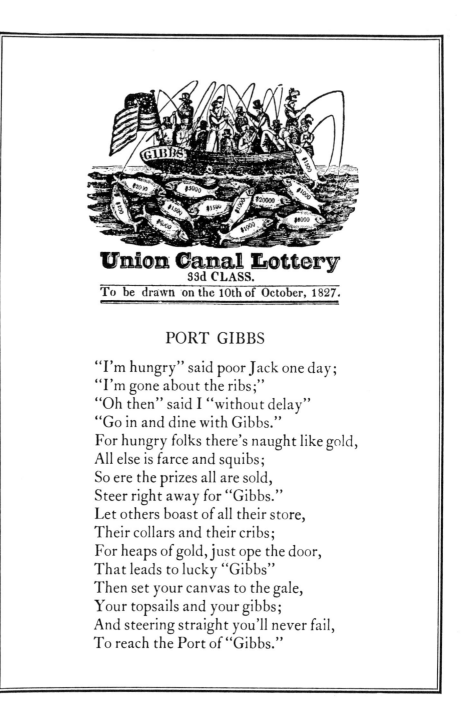

Union Canal Lottery
33d CLASS.
To be drawn on the 10th of October, 1827.

PORT GIBBS

"I'm hungry" said poor Jack one day;
"I'm gone about the ribs;"
"Oh then" said I "without delay"
"Go in and dine with Gibbs."
For hungry folks there's naught like gold,
All else is farce and squibs;
So ere the prizes all are sold,
Steer right away for "Gibbs."
Let others boast of all their store,
Their collars and their cribs;
For heaps of gold, just ope the door,
That leads to lucky "Gibbs"
Then set your canvas to the gale,
Your topsails and your gibbs;
And steering straight you'll never fail,
To reach the Port of "Gibbs."

A nineteenth-century lottery handbill. "Gibbs" refers to a noted ticket seller of the day.

By Chance a Winner

THE HISTORY OF LOTTERIES

George Sullivan

Illustrated with photographs and reproductions

DODD, MEAD & COMPANY · NEW YORK

Acknowledgments

Many people were helpful in providing source material, photographs, lottery tickets, and reproductions of tickets for use in this book. Special thanks are offered Norman F. Gallman, Commissioner of Taxation & Finance, State of New York; Ralph Batch, Director, New Jersey State Lottery; Edward J. Powers, Executive Director, New Hampshire Sweepstakes Commission; Ted Browne, Fuller, Smith & Ross, Inc., New York; Kenneth J. Coffey, Public Information Officer, Selective Service System; Paul Hughes, Littlewoods Pools, Liverpool; Dr. R. Merz, Secretary General, International Association of State Lotteries, Zurich; Hidemasa Uemura, Chief, Enterprise Division, Bureau of Finance, Tokyo Metropolitan Government; Roger W. Fromm, New York State Historical Association; Rare Book Division, New York Public Library; William J. Sullivan and J. Harry Tiernan III.

Contents

1

"A Testimony of My Affection for Him"

In October, 1970, a sixty-one-year-old Detroit typewriter repairman named Charles Klotz, vacationing in Niagara Falls, New York, made a $3.00 purchase that was to transform his life. What he bought was a slip of paper about the size of a dollar bill—a New York State Lottery ticket.

Klotz tucked the ticket into his billfold and all but forgot it until one evening several weeks later when he received a telephone call from New York Lottery officials telling him that his ticket was one of fourteen that had been drawn, making him eligible for a second drawing for the grand prize.

"Would you like to come to New York City to be present for the drawing?" he was asked.

Klotz didn't hesitate. "You bet!" he answered.

The fateful day was January 28, 1971. The scene was the main concourse of Grand Central Terminal. Slightly more than five hundred people were on hand, when, shortly after noon, a blindfolded official reached into a large goldfish bowl containing cards representing races already run in a given week at a New

Buying lottery tickets in New York City.

Charles Klotz says this horse-shoe brought him lottery luck.

York track. The results of the race selected were to be used to determine the amounts won by the grand prize ticket holders.

Klotz heard the fourth place winner announced, then the third place, then second. "And now," said the man at the microphone, "the winner of the grand prize. It's post position number four!"

"Mine! It's mine!" Klotz screamed, and he jumped to his feet.

Charles Klotz had reason to be excited. He had just won $50,000 a year for the next twenty years—one million dollars.

Scenes like this have been taking place with ever-increasing frequency in recent years as more and more states adopt legal lotteries as a form of taxation. Countless state legislators have come to look upon the lottery as a painless method of providing sorely needed funds, and the majority of hard-pressed taxpayers go along with the idea. Seldom are the prizes as high as a million dollars, but in almost every case the amounts are enough to change a person's life overnight.

New Hampshire established the first state-sponsored lottery of modern times in 1964. Three years later New York launched its lottery. New Jersey followed New York. By early 1972, more than a dozen other states were considering establishing lotteries of their own.

What is a lottery? It is any prize contest based entirely on chance, and which requires entrants to pay a fee or buy something to take part. In its simplest form, a lottery might involve one hundred players, each of whom buys a numbered $1.00 ticket. Corresponding numbers are put into a container, shaken, and one drawn out at random. The owner of the drawn ticket wins the $100 pool.

Nathan Proller, a commissioner of the New York State Lottery, draws a winner.

States use the lottery concept to their benefit by holding back a portion of the pool. For example, New York State keeps 45 per cent of all lottery income, using it for primary, secondary, and higher education, and providing college scholarships. Another 40 per cent of what is received goes into the prize fund. The balance is used for administrative expenses.

There is nothing new about lotteries. They date to the most ancient of times.

The word "lot," which refers to an object used in deciding a matter of chance, is believed to be Teutonic in origin. It is derived from *hleut*, which designated a pebble, bean, or similar token used to divide property or settle disputes. Other cultures had terms that were similar in meaning and sound. In Middle English and Old English, the word was *hlot*; in Dutch it was *lot*; in Danish, *lod*. The Romance languages contributed *loterie*, which is French, and *lotteria*, which is Italian.

The Old Testament reports the use of the lot on many occasions, either in the form of casting it on the ground or drawing it from a vessel of some type. Land was divided by lot. It was the method used to solve political and labor problems. The first king of Israel was chosen by lot.

In the New Testament, casting lots was a method of ascertaining the divine will. Stones of different colors or with special symbols inscribed were placed in a vessel and shaken until one popped out. This method of selection seemed to remove the human element; God was making the choice. Following the death of Judas Iscariot, the casting of lots determined that Matthias, not Joseph, should be named his successor as an apostle. "And they prayed," according to Acts 1:24, "and said, 'Lord . . . show which one of these two thou hast chosen to take the place in this ministry . . .' And they cast lots . . . and the lot fell on Matthias."

Dice for the casting of lots, and for gaming, too, were used by the Egyptians, Assyrians, Greeks, and Romans. Dice of Roman times were of several different types. Some were small cubes of bone or stone, marked on each surface like modern dice with a number of small dots, varying from one to six. Another type had fourteen different polished surfaces of equal size, each marked with a Roman numeral from one to fourteen. Still others took the form of a small strip of bone or ivory, slightly larger than a paper match of the present day. Etched into one of the two flat surfaces of the strip was the word "victor."

At Roman banquets, and in connection with other forms of revelry, guests were often awarded gifts of lot. After the fall of Rome, feudal princes of Europe continued the custom, but adapted the idea as a source of profit. Venice had a government monopoly on lotteries, using them as a form of taxation. Sixteenth-century Venetian merchants, and those in Florence and Genoa, too, distributed lottery tickets to their customers, then held drawings to determine prize winners.

Francis I of France established a government *loterie* in 1539. In time, this method of raising money came to play a vital role in France's fiscal policy. This was especially true after the French people, revolted by the unrestrained spending on the part of their monarchs, refused to pay their surging taxes. The War of the Spanish Succession was financed by public lotteries.

Lotteries also began to thrive in England about this time. Queen Elizabeth chartered a lottery in 1566 which provided for the selling of 40,000 tickets, which were priced at ten shillings apiece, for prizes that consisted of "plate and certaine sorts of merchaundizes."

Lottery tickets were sold in England as a means of subsidizing the first American colonists. Later, the colonies themselves sponsored and authorized lotteries—to finance the construction of churches and schools, and the building of bridges, roads, lighthouses, and port facilities. Several colonies relied upon lotteries to finance their responsibilities in the French and Indian War.

ABOVE: *A French ticket seller of the mid-eighteenth century.*

RIGHT: *Lottery advertising took this form in England during the 1820's.*

Congress, in 1776, sought to raise more than a million dollars by national lottery "in support of troops in the field." It was a failure.

People of the highest stature were involved in lotteries. During September, 1793, George Washington, then in his second term as President, wrote a warm and affectionate letter to one Tobias Lear, a young man of twenty-nine, who had recently ended a period of seven years as Washington's private secretary.

Lear's wife had died several weeks before. The father had taken the couple's only son, two-and-one-half-year-old Benjamin Lincoln Lear, to Portsmouth, New Hampshire, to live with the mother of his deceased wife.

Washington knew young Benjamin well, for he had been born in the President's home in Philadelphia and had gone on living there with his parents. The President's letter to Benjamin's father revealed his tender feelings for the child. He referred to Benjamin as "our little favourite," and expressed the wish "that he may always be as charming and as promising as he now is . . .

"As a testimony of my affection for him," the President's letter said, "I send him a Ticket in the lottery which is now drawing in the Federal City."

Alexander Hamilton, the first Secretary of the Treasury, who planned and put into being many of our nation's essential fiscal policies, wrote interestingly about lotteries. Among Hamilton's papers in the Library of Congress are two sheets in his hand entitled "Ideas for a Lottery." According to Hamilton, a lottery to be successful had to have two basic characteristics. The first was simplicity; the scheme had to be easily understood by the prospective ticket purchasers so as to present "fewer obstacles between hope and gratification." The second requirement was low-priced tickets. Said Hamilton: "Every body, almost, can and will be willing to hazard a trifling sum for the chance of considerable gain . . ."

In the century that followed the ratification of the Constitu-

7

Governor William T. Cahill officiates at a lottery drawing in New Jersey . . .

. . . and Governor John W. King in New Hampshire.

tion, lotteries skyrocketed in popularity. Ticket vendors became more numerous than blacksmiths, ticket agencies more common than taverns. Philadelphia, in 1833, had more than two hundred offices devoted to the selling of lottery tickets.

But as lotteries climbed in popularity, so did the scandal and corruption that had come to be associated with them. The evildoing culminated in the Louisiana Lottery, which spread its tentacles to every corner of the nation. It is a dismal chapter in American history.

Indignant and angered citizens took their grievances to state and federal lawmakers, and in the final decades of the eighteenth century, a great wave of legislation was enacted which served to outlaw virtually all lottery activity.

This legislation remained in effect until very recent times. Now the luster is being restored to the legal lottery, and state lawmakers are repealing statutes which banned lottery activity. The whir of spinning wheels and the sharp click of turning plastic capsules may soon be familiar sounds to Americans everywhere.

Interestingly, government-run lotteries thrive in every part of the world. They are a basic form of taxation in virtually every Latin-American country. They are in widespread use throughout Europe; in England they are almost a way of life. Lotteries flourish in several African countries, in Japan and Australia.

The use of the lottery is not limited to state or national governments and their tax-raising authorities. Lotteries are common to the American social and cultural scene on many different levels. The federal government selects the order in which young men will be called into military service by means of a lottery. It has done so for more than a century. Names pulled from a lottery wheel determined who would serve in the Union ranks during the Civil War. Jury members are often selected in the same manner.

Bingo, a form of money-raising used by many churches, is a type of lottery. So are raffles, tickets for which are sold in every

9

"Punch Bowl" and . . .

. . . *"Wheel of Fortune"* are two common games based on the lottery principle.

city and town in the United States. Pick up a national magazine and count the number of advertisements for "sweepstakes." These are lotteries, too.

Several different kinds of lotteries are common to state fairs, county fairs, street festivals, and lawn parties. "Punch Bowl" is one. Pay a fee, usually 25 cents, and pick out a four-digit number from a goldfish bowl. Your hope is that it matches one of the numbered prizes.

The wheel of fortune is very common. In this, you bet a small sum, usually 10 or 25 cents, on which number a spinning wheel will stop. This game is a first cousin to roulette, wherein players bet on which slot of a wheel a small ball will come to rest in.

Now state governments are rediscovering the lottery as a revenue-raising device. Millions of Americans are investing their pocket money on a regular basis in an effort to reap the same good fortune as Charles Klotz. And soon many millions more will be able to do so.

2

The Lottery in
Colonial America

America's experience with lotteries dates to the
earliest colonial period, to the beleaguered settlement at Jamestown, Virginia. Founded in 1607, Jamestown was subjected to
every type of adversity—disease, dissension, Indian siege, fire,
and famine. Income from the colony was virtually nil. Little
wonder that the merchant group that organized the settlement,
the Virginia Company of London, found it increasingly difficult
to support Jamestown financially.

In the spring of 1612, the Virginia Company petitioned the
king for relief and was granted a new charter, one that empow-
ered the company to conduct "one or more lottery or lotteries, to
have continuance, and to endure and be held for the space of
one whole year . . ." The drawings were to be held in England,
and the prizes were to be whatever the company "in their discre-
tion shall see convenient."

To stir up interest in the venture, the Virginia Company had
handbills printed and distributed, and a lively ballad was com-
posed hailing the merits of the enterprise. The ballad's twenty-
six stanzas acclaimed the lottery not so much for its prize list,
but for its nobility and Christian purpose. This stanza is typical:

It is to plant a Kingdome sure,
   where savadge people dwell;
God will favour Christians still,
   and like the purpose well.
Take courage then with willingnesse,
   let hands and hearts agree:
A braver enterprize then this,
   I thinke can never bee.

Tickets were sold in the large cities of England and the first prize-winning numbers were drawn in the summer of 1612. Stow's *Chronicle*, a newspaper of the day, stated, "This lottery was so plainly carried and honestly performed that it gave full satisfaction to all persons." Two of the first three winning tickets were held by Anglican churches, evidence of the widespread approval that the enterprise had gained.

The Virginia Company sponsored and promoted other lotteries in England over the next few years, and the income they provided helped to sustain the Jamestown settlement and also finance the sending of more colonists there. How very important the lottery was to Jamestown can be seen from these figures: In the fiscal year 1620-1621, the Virginia Company estimated its total expenses to be £17,800; lotteries were expected to provide almost half this amount—£8,000.

However, these expectations were never realized. In the spring of 1620, almost without warning, the House of Commons ordered an end to the selling of tickets. Angry discord among the officers of the Virginia Company was one reason the ban was instituted. There were accusations that Company money was being misappropriated. There was another reason. The House of Commons felt the Virginia Company had no right to conduct lotteries because they had never been given the privilege by Parliament.

Whatever the reason, the ban was a sharp blow for the Virginia Company and its struggling colony. Possibly no other pioneer group suffered so many and varied setbacks as did the

persons who chose to settle Jamestown, and the abrupt abolish-
ment of their chief means of financial sustenance was not the
least of them.

England at this time was awash with lotteries, both private and
government sponsored. According to John Ashton, in *A History
of English Lotteries*, published in London in 1898, lottery tickets
were sold by newsstand proprietors, hat makers, snuff merchants,
eating-house proprietors, barbers, bakers, and shoeblacks. Itin-
erant merchants, who dealt in these and a wide range of other
goods and services, also served as ticket sellers. It was natural
that lotteries would be well known in colonial America. Like tea-
drinking and church-going, and most other customs and conven-
tions of the time, the idea of the lottery was transplanted from
the old continent to the new.

Lotteries were often employed when a person wanted to dispose of his household goods or his land. It was an assured method
of getting a fair price for one's holdings. No less a figure than
Thomas Jefferson wrote approvingly of lotteries in this regard.
"An article of property," said Jefferson, ". . . is sometimes of so
large a value as that no purchaser can be found while the owner
owes debts, has no other means of payment, and his creditors no
other chance of obtaining it but by its sale at a full and fair
price. The lottery is here a salutory instrument for disposing of
it . . ."

The Delaware Lottery was used by William Alexander (Lord Stirling)
to dispose of his land holdings in New York and New Jersey.

14

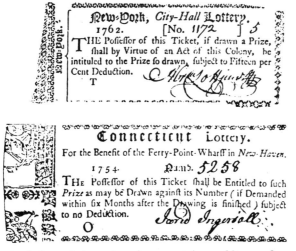

Money raised through lotteries often went for public works projects.

In 1719, one Joseph Marion of Boston sold one hundred lottery tickets at five pounds each, advertising their availability in
newspapers of the day. Two brick houses were the prizes Marion
offered. Philadelphia's *American Weekly Mercury* for February
23, 1720, carried an announcement for a lottery with 350 tickets
priced at twenty shillings apiece, with a "new brick house, corner

of Third and Arch streets," as the prize. Silver teapots, jewelry, and books were typical of prizes of lesser value that were offered.

Newspapers of the day carried notices of lotteries, giving historians a good idea of the number of lotteries and the many different types. For instance, advertisements in New Jersey newspapers of the 1720's announced lotteries for the purpose of purchasing a brick steeple and bells for a church in Burlington; raising money to build a boat landing at Raritan, and another to pay the debts of one Peter Cochran, who was languishing in prison because of them.

In Pennsylvania, before the legislature finally succeeded in putting a ban on private lotteries, no less than fifty-two of them were being conducted. Most were quite public-spirited in nature, and meant to raise funds for schools, bridges, roads, church buildings, and the like.

One of the most noted of Pennsylvania lotteries of this period earned funds for the "College, Academy and Charitable School of Philadelphia," which later became the University of Pennsylvania. At one period, nine different lotteries were contributing to this enterprise.

The method of operation followed a set pattern. A group of citizens would petition the General Assembly for permission to conduct a lottery, presenting its "scheme," or plan. After authorizing the lottery, the legislature would set down rules the enter-

Churches frequently sponsored lotteries, too.

16

prise had to follow. Directors and managers for the lottery were appointed. In Pennsylvania, a manager had to take an oath not to seek a prize for himself or any other person, and to combat "any undue or sinister practice." Later managers were bonded to protect against fraud.

The next step was to print the ticket books. Each page of each book contained several horizontal rows of tickets, three identical tickets to a row. Each ticket was imprinted with the advice that, "This ticket entitles the bearer to such prize as may be drawn against its number if demanded in nine months after the drawing is finished, subject to such deductions as mentioned in the scheme."

When a person made a purchase, the outer ticket in the horizontal row was clipped out of the book, signed by the seller, and handed to the buyer. When all the tickets in the outside column of a page had been sold, the tickets in the middle column were snipped out of the book, rolled up individually, and "made fast with thread or silk." These were deposited in a big sealed box. The column of tickets that remained in the book was used for comparison should a mistake occur or suspected fraud arise.

On the day of the drawing, the managers assembled at a public room. The box containing the rolled-up tickets was opened and they were carefully mixed. Then an "indifferent and fit person" was selected to draw the winning numbers.

Usually two boxes were used instead of merely one. The first box contained the numbered tickets, duplicates of the tickets that had been sold. The second box contained still another set of tickets. Each of these was either printed with a description of the prize it would bring or it was blank. The prize-winning tickets, which sometimes totaled close to half the number sold, were referred to as "fortunates." The others were called "blanks."

On the day of the drawing, a person would select a numbered ticket from the first box. It would be unrolled and the number read aloud. Then another person would select a ticket from the

A sequence of tickets in the Perth Amboy Lottery of 1761.

second box. This told whether the first ticket had won a prize. If it was a "fortunate," the number and amount of the prize were recorded. The drawing continued until all the tickets had been drawn.

Sometimes the prize list would total 85 per cent of the total monies realized from the sale of tickets. The 15 per cent was retained by the lottery sponsors, but this ratio was subject to variation. The amount of time the managers were granted to sell tickets also varied. Sometimes it was a year, other times more or less than a year. Toward the end of the 1700's, rotating drums, or lottery wheels, began to replace the boxes.

At first there was no objection to lotteries, but little by little criticism began to build. The Mathers of Massachusetts, Increase and his son, Cotton, both Congregational clergymen and authors,

18

opposed lotteries for reasons of morality. Cotton Mather, in a diary entry dated July 30, 1690, wrote: "Understanding that many, especially of our young People gave themselves a *Liberty*, to do Things not of *good Report*, especially, in using the scandalous Games of *Lottery* I sett myself . . . against their Miscarriages . . ."

At least partly because of Mather, Congregational ministers met at Boston in 1699 and, as a group, condemned lotteries, but not so much for their lack of morality as for the small return they gave in contrast to the large sums collected. The ministers called them "a plain cheat upon the people."

The Society of Friends, the Quakers, also opposed lotteries, as they did all forms of gambling, most types of amusements, and some forms of art. But the Quakers had little influence on most of colonial America. Indeed, Quaker preachers were fined, flogged, and even hanged in the Massachusetts Bay Colony, and Quakers in general were only able to establish scattered settlements.

The conspicious exception was Pennsylvania where William Penn, in 1681, established a haven for Quakers from England. From the very first, these early Quaker settlers sought to outlaw lotteries. The first General Assembly of Pennsylvania, which met in 1682, and which was dominated by members of the Quaker sect, passed the "Great Law," a section of which declared "That if any person be Convicted of playing at Cards, Dice, Lotteries . . . such persons shall, for every such offense, pay five shillings, or Suffer five Days Imprisonment (at hard labour) in the house of Correction."

However, the English sovereigns, William and Mary, nullified the act in 1693. And when Quaker legislators passed other anti-lottery laws in 1693, 1700, and 1705, these likewise were overturned by the British rulers.

It was not the Quakers nor the Mathers that triggered the decline of lotteries during the period, but the lotteries themselves.

19

As the lotteries continued to spiral in popularity, sponsors and promoters were found to be acting in bad faith. Some were wholly dishonest.

Corrupt promoters controlled the drawings so that tickets for the most valuable prizes were never drawn, or they cluttered the prize list with inferior merchandise. The practice of a promoter fleeing a town without ever holding a drawing was not uncommon.

Merchants of the day were another factor. They saw lotteries as a form of competition, one that soaked up money that might otherwise be available for the purchase of goods and services.

Local governments began to consider lottery regulation. Legislators cited the harmful effect lottery schemes had upon the poor, who were deemed the chief purchasers of tickets. The Massachusetts General Court, in 1719, thundered against lotteries as tempting "the Children and the Servants of several Gentlemen, Merchants and Traders and other unwary People . . . into a vain and foolish Expence of money." In 1747, in the Royal Province of New York, lotteries were denounced because they encouraged "Numbers of Laboring People to Assemble at Taverns where such Lotteries are usually Set on Foot and drawn."

New York and Massachusetts were among the first states to prohibit all lotteries that did not have legislative approval. Similar legislation was passed in Connecticut. Private lotteries were banned in Rhode Island beginning in 1733.

Pennsylvania managed finally to put an effective ban on lotteries, except those authorized by the Pennsylvania legislature or the British government, in 1762. The law prescribed a fine of £500 to be levied on anyone who organized a private lottery.

Virginia was more tolerant toward lotteries than the other colonies. While legislation was passed that outlawed all except government-approved lotteries, it came much later. The eminence of those involved in lotteries in Virginia was surely a factor. George Washington was a frequent ticket buyer and he also served as a lottery patron. William Fairfax, George Mason, and

Colonel William Fitzhugh were other Virginia notables whose names were associated with lotteries.

The popularity of lotteries continued through the later years of the colonial period, but with the distinction that they were licensed lotteries, approved by the local colonial government and often operated for its benefit.

It would have been almost as difficult for legislatures to forego lottery activity as for the federal government of the present day to attempt to do without the income tax or any other major source of revenue. Most of the colonial governments were in urgent need of funds, largely because of the general financial instability of the period. Colonial America was mainly an agricultural society; there was only a very limited amount of manufacturing. Hard goods had to be imported, resulting in an unfavorable balance of trade with England. If colonial governments could have issued letters of credit, the problem would have been eased, but the British would not permit this. As a result, the colonies were almost always short of money, as were their citizens, who were heated in their opposition to higher taxes.

In some colonies the need for income was particularly pressing. Virginia's first legislatively-sponsored lottery, conducted in 1754, was intended to raise £6,000 to build fortifications against the French. This was the period of the French and Indian War, and Virginia planters were skirmishing with French colonists for

Massachusetts-LOTTERY, (No. One.) May 1758.

THE Poffeffor of this Ticket [No. 049.] fhall be intitled to any Prize drawn against faid Number, in a LOTTERY granted by an Act of the General Court of the Province aforefaid, paffed in April 1758, towards fupplying the Treafury with a Sum of Money for the intended Expedition against Canada, fubject to no Deduction, E

Massachusetts used a lottery to raise funds to support its participation in the French and Indian War.

21

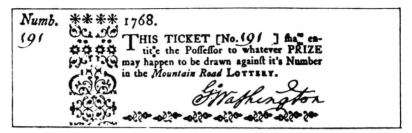

A ticket for the Mountain Road Lottery.

land rights along the Ohio River. Massachusetts also turned to a lottery to finance its participation in the war. When New York held its first lottery in 1746, it planned to use the money to fortify the city of New York.

Fully one-third of the lotteries of this period were for internal improvements, for repairing bridges or building roads. A good number of others were church-sponsored, while still others were for the benefit of schools or colleges.

One lottery of the time was known as the Mountain Road Lottery. Its sponsor was George Washington. About fifty tickets for this lottery bearing Washington's signature are in the hands of historians and collectors.

The purpose of the Mountain Road Lottery was to raise funds to construct a road over the Allegheny Mountains which would link the Ohio River with Tidewater Virginia, where Washington had real estate holdings. The road would thus serve to increase the value of the land.

This is the explanation usually given for Washington's participation in the lottery. Philip G. Nordell, a leading expert on American lotteries, has another theory. He has noted that advertisements promoting the lottery stated that its purpose was "to make a road over the mountain to the warm and hot springs in Augusta County." Washington, in his own records, referred to the enterprise as the "Warm Spring Lottery."

Why would George Washington have a special interest in the warm and bubbling waters of Augusta County? Nordell points

22

out that Washington's stepdaughter, twelve-year-old Patsy Curtis, was the victim of convulsive seizures (from which she was to die in 1773). The springs on the other side of the Alleghenies were believed to have curative powers, but the trails over the mountains were impassable to the horse-drawn vehicles of the time. Washington, says Nordell, initiated the lottery in order to open a road for Patsy's sake.

Whatever Washington's motive in establishing the lottery, the enterprise was not a success. Most of the tickets went unsold, so no drawing was ever held.

Washington was a meticulous record-keeper, and his papers reveal the attention he gave to lotteries over the years. He won a parcel of land in the Colonel Byrd raffle, the sum of five pounds in the Strothers Lottery of 1763, and he showed a profit of sixteen pounds in the York Lottery in 1766.

Some lotteries had unusual purposes. Connecticut held a lottery to raise money to pay the owners of a house that had been set afire while occupied by British troops. Connecticut also used a lottery to raise £700 to replace money taken by a tax collector in Colchester. Massachusetts advertised a lottery in 1757 for the purpose of rebuilding a glass bottle factory in Germantown which had been destroyed by fire. New Jersey held three annual drawings beginning in 1759 to raise a total of £1800 to pay Indian land claims.

Massachusetts supported several lotteries in the early to mid-1760's to rebuild Faneuil Hall which had been gutted by fire. A gift to the town of Boston from the merchant Peter Faneuil, Faneuil Hall was to win renown as the "Cradle of Liberty" for the stirring speeches made there on behalf of the American Revolution.

One of the Faneuil Hall Lotteries aimed to collect $12,000 through the sale of tickets, returning to winning ticket holders $10,800 in prize money. The Boston *Gazette* for November 1, 1762, gave this breakdown for the awarding of prizes:

23

1	prize of	1,000	is	1,000 dollars
1	" "	500	is	500 "
2	prizes of	200	are	400 dollars
12	" "	100	is	1,200 "
20	" "	50	is	1,000 "
20	" "	20	is	400 "
30	" "	10	is	300 "
200	" "	6	is	1,200 "
1200	" "	4	is	4,800 "

1486 Prizes	10,800
6000 Tickets at 2 dollars each is	$12,000
To be paid as prizes	$10,800
Remains for the use of Faneuil Hall	$1,200

The managers of the Faneuil Hall Lottery included many men who were in the forefront of Revolutionary activity in Massachusetts, including John Scollay, Benjamin Austin, and Thomas Cushing. Some of the tickets bore John Hancock's sprawling signature.

King's College in New York, later known as Columbia Univer-

Faneuil Hall rebuilt; original size of the structure is shown in outline.

24

John Hancock signed this Faneuil Hall lottery ticket.

sity, was the first college to seek funding by means of a lottery. In 1746 the New York Assembly granted the college a license to raise £2,250. It was the first of five lotteries King's College held over the ensuing nine years.

Other prestigious colleges of the present day were originally funded, at least in part, by lotteries. The very first lottery to win the approval of the Connecticut Assembly was for the benefit of Yale. Granted in 1747, the license permitted Yale to raise £7,500 for student housing, but only about two-thirds of that amount was actually realized.

The College of New Jersey, now known as Princeton University, also sought to raise money by means of a lottery, but New Jersey legislators refused to grant the college a license for it. The college reacted by petitioning the Connecticut Assembly for the right to hold a lottery in that colony. In 1753, in a bright burst of neighborliness, the license was granted, giving the College of New Jersey the right to raise £2,000, with the drawing to be held in Stamford. Not until 1762 was Princeton permitted to conduct a lottery in New Jersey.

Harvard College, too, tried a lottery as a means of raising funds, but the venture was less than successful. The college did not win the approval of the Massachusetts legislature until late in the colonial period, in 1765. Sanction was granted for the raising of £3,200 for the construction of student housing.

25

A receipt for tickets in the Newcastle Lottery.

This was a time of turmoil and strife in Massachusetts. The British were seeking financial means to support an army of ten thousand men to defend the colonies against the still hostile French in newly conquered Canada, and from Indian attacks as well. The principal method devised to raise this money was the Stamp Act, a form of taxation. Proposed in 1764 and passed into law the next year, the Stamp Act required tax stamps to be placed on all legal and commercial papers, pamphlets, newspapers, and even almanacs.

With the passage of the Stamp Act, the storm clouds began to gather. Harvard's lottery was one victim of the turbulence. By 1775 many tickets still remained to be sold, and school officials voted to purchase two thousand chances if that amount remained unsold at the time of the drawing. What finally happened is set down in the college records: "The managers of the aforesaid Lottery afterw'd gave it up, the war breaking out."

Other lotteries of this time suffered similar difficulties. New Jersey attempted to raise £500 in 1765 to straighten the road between New York and Philadelphia. The *New York Journal* of December 18, 1766, carried the announcement that the lottery had been postponed because of "the troubled State of Affairs . . . occasioned by the Stamp Act."

But the general tumult of the period was not the only problem. The British government had developed a growing disfavor toward colonial lotteries. As early as 1761, England's Lords of Trade had objected to the raising of money by this means, ex-

26

pressing the opinion that the means of regulation were not strict enough. Later, the Lords of Trade were to condemn a Philadelphia lottery because it introduced a spirit of "dissipation prejudicial to the Fortunes of Individuals, and the Interest of the Public."

Thus, it probably came as no surprise when, in 1769, a circular letter was distributed to the governors of Massachusetts, New Hampshire, New York, New Jersey, North Carolina, South Carolina, Virginia, Georgia, Delaware, Pennsylvania, and West Florida directing them not to authorize any lottery without the permission of the Crown. The letter sharply denounced lotteries, declaring, "such practice doth tend to disengage those who become adventurers therein from the spirit of industry and attention to their proper callings and occupations on which the public welfare so greatly depends . . ." The letter took note of the proliferation of private lotteries and accused them of "great frauds and abuses."

For several years after the issuance of the letter, lottery activity was limited to Rhode Island (which holds the distinction of conducting more lotteries than any other colony), Connecticut, and Maryland, colonies whose charters did not compel them to accept the ban. Delaware, which had withdrawn from Pennsylvania and declared itself a separate political entity, chose not to obey the order, and also continued to hold lotteries. Pennsylvania itself, although a proprietary colony, wherein a proprietor, the Penn family, held governing power, had to accept the letter's instructions.

There can be no doubt about it—lotteries were an essential form of financing in the later colonial period. John Ezell, in his definitive book on the subject, *Fortune's Merry Wheel; The Lottery in America,* found that 158 lottery licenses were granted in the thirty-year period beginning in 1744. Every colony, and surely virtually every citizen, had experience with lotteries, and if there was any serious opposition to this form of money-raising at this time, historians are unaware of it.

27

3

The Golden Age

In the early stages of the Revolutionary War, British strategy was well known—to gain control of the Hudson River, dividing the colonies in two. General Washington, aware of this plan, shifted his forces from Boston to New York, stationing them in Brooklyn and Manhattan.

On August 27, 1776, in the Battle of Long Island, the British under General William Howe routed Washington's Brooklyn force, and then proceeded to drive the colonial troops northward and out of Manhattan. Washington's defensive plan was to keep inshore from Howe and to launch counterstrikes whenever the opportunity arose. This Washington did with brilliance later that year at Trenton and at Princeton in January, 1777.

But General Howe and his red-coated forces were not the greatest problem the colonies faced. Money was; specifically, how to raise the funds necessary to finance the war.

Taxation was virtually out of the question. The colonists had a deep-seated hatred of taxation in any and all forms. Besides, since there was no well-established central government, there was no machinery to collect taxes or enforce tax legislation.

To solve the problem of finances, the Continental Congress issued paper money, great volumes of it. Following the hostilities at Bunker Hill and up until November 29, 1779, paper money in the amount of $241,552,380 gushed from government presses. Each state was allotted a specified amount to redeem. Almost immediately inflation became rampant. By 1780, the value of Continental currency in silver had fallen to forty to one, and the expression "not worth a Continental" had come into widespread use.

The Continental Congress also sought to raise money by borrowing it, both from domestic and foreign sources. France espe-

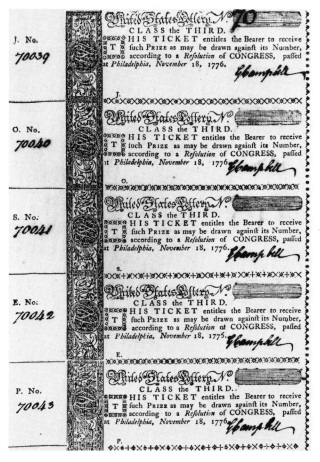

The "United States Lottery" was meant to provide funds to support the Revolutionary War. This is a page from a ticket book.

(Courtesy of The New York Historical Society, New York City)

29

cially, and Spain and Holland, too, were cooperative in this regard.

The lottery was a third method. On November 1, 1776, the Board of the Treasury announced a plan to raise $1,005,000 for the support of the Colonial Army by means of a huge lottery involving the sale of 100,000 tickets—42,317 fortunates and 57,683 blanks. There were to be four separate "classes," or divisions, each with prizes ranging from $20.00 to $50,000. Holders of winning tickets in excess of $50.00 were to be paid in treasury bank notes, these to be redeemable after five years at an interest rate of 4 per cent.

Tickets of the first class sold briskly, but tickets for the later drawings did not. Books of tickets were sent to the various state governors with the request that the states make wholesale purchases, but the plan was not received with enthusiasm. Massachusetts, for example, at first agreed to purchase nine hundred tickets, but later reconsidered, offering its allotment for sale to the general public.

The second, third, and fourth classes were only partially sold, and drawings were postponed time and again. No one knows for certain how much money was realized from ticket sales; in those frantic times, careful record-keeping was not the order of the day. But it is known that the total amount earned was substantially less than the $1,005,000 hoped for. The best that can be said about the government's first attempt at a national lottery was that it provided a temporary reservoir of funds that could be drawn upon.

Some state governments also sponsored lotteries to raise money in support of the war effort. In 1778, Massachusetts sought to earn $750,000 to "reward enlistments," and two years later the state attempted to raise £20,400 to help clothe Massachusetts soldiers. New York, Vermont, and Rhode Island also held lotteries in support of the military cause.

Interestingly, most of the lotteries conducted by the states dur-

The Continental Congress sought to raise funds in support of the Revolutionary War by means of a lottery; this is the cover and title page of the lottery ticket book.

ing the time of the American Revolution were meant for the benefit of state projects. Rather than provide funds for the American military, Connecticut preferred to repair a paper mill in Hartford, Massachusetts to build a road from Westfield to Great

Barrington, and New York to purchase a supply of fire buckets.

During the postwar period, Congress again became involved with a lottery, one of an unusual type. John Adams, United States minister to Holland, was seeking to negotiate a loan from the Dutch. America's poor credit standing, plus the tight money situation that prevailed, made Adams' task a difficult one. He finally had to agree to pay the Dutch a bonus of 690,000 guilders on a 4 per cent, two-million-guilder loan. The bonus was to be paid in United States notes, which were to be distributed by lot to those among the Dutch who would agree to lend money. In a letter to Benjamin Franklin, Adams expressed the fear that the terms of the loan were so unfavorable to the United States that they might serve to discredit him, but he declared that conditions were such that he had no other course.

The decades that followed the Revolutionary War were ones of surging growth for the United States. The census of 1790 showed New York's population to be 340,120. By 1810, the figure had jumped to 959,049. In the same period, Kentucky went from 73,677 to 406,511, and Pennsylvania from 434,373 to 810,081. Other states showed increases, too.

This enormous growth triggered demands from citizens of the day for additional services. They wanted roads and canals to get goods to market, water and sewage systems, and fire-fighting equipment.

When a state seeks to provide such services nowadays, it usually finances them out of tax revenues or borrows the money by issuing bonds. But in the 1790's and over the decades that followed, the idea of raising money by taxation remained in great disfavor and, overall, was a slow, laborious process. As for bonds, there was no well-established system of public credit that would permit local or state governments to raise money in this fashion. Lotteries were the tried and proven method.

From 1783, the year that saw the ending of the Revolutionary War, until 1790, about one hundred different lotteries were held

32

in the United States. Massachusetts, Rhode Island, and Virginia sponsored about half of them.

As new states were established, they, too, turned to lotteries to raise money. A lottery was authorized by Tennessee in 1823 for a hospital in Nashville; Frankfort, Kentucky, was granted a franchise in 1838 to raise $50,000 for a water supply system. Even the territorial governments relied upon lotteries. Missouri's first lottery, in 1817, was to provide fire-fighting equipment for the city of St. Louis, and the Michigan Territory authorized Detroit to conduct a lottery in 1819 for the same purpose.

The biggest sums raised by lotteries during this period went toward building up the nation's transportation system. As the population increased and the push westward began, improved roads were needed. Bridges had to be built and streams and rivers dredged so as to be serviceable as canals. Scores of lottery charters were granted for these purposes.

Massachusetts, for example, granted lottery authorizations for such projects as the Hatfield Bridge, a road from Ipswich to Gloucester, the South Hadley Canal, and the biggest project of all, the Springfield Bridge over the Connecticut River, a $30,000 enterprise. Other states had similar lotteries. One of the largest ever up to this time sought to raise $400,000 for the construction of canals and locks between the Schuylkill and Delaware Rivers, and the Schuylkill and Susquehanna Rivers.

Harvard College tried fund-raising by lottery many times.

33

Churches and schools benefited, too. No less than fourteen states granted franchises to religious groups, including every major denomination with the exception of the Quakers.

Harvard University, which had tried a lottery in 1772 and saw it fail because of the oncoming war, tried a second time in 1794. This time Harvard's hope was for £8,000. Rhode Island College, later known as Brown University, turned to a lottery in 1795. Massachusetts allowed lottery tickets for the benefit of Dartmouth to be sold within its borders.

New York authorized a $200,000 lottery for the aid of Union College. Rival Columbia College objected heatedly to the bill's passage. To appease Columbia, the state of New York gave the College a tract of land known as the Hosack Botanical Gardens as a site for a new campus. This land is now a twenty-one acre tract in midtown New York and includes the land on which Rockefeller Center is built. It is the principal source of Columbia's wealth.

The University of North Carolina utilized a lottery in 1801 to complete construction of its main buildings. The Visitors of Central College, later the University of Virginia, voted in 1817 to sponsor a lottery but never followed through on the plan.

Small schools benefited, too. Georgia ran more than a score of lotteries to aid county academies, and Mississippi authorized eight lotteries for pre-college education.

These are only a sampling. In the fifty years before the Civil War, schools and colleges in the United States benefited from more than three hundred lotteries. These enterprises thus made a significant contribution to the early development of the American education system.

All the while, lotteries were also being conducted for individuals, for private gain—to subsidize a new industry, to pay a person's debts, or, as in the case of New York, for the Society for the Relief of Poor Widows, or Pennsylvania's lottery for the "useful arts."

34

A blindfolded boy draws tickets from the wheel in this Baltimore lottery of the 1850's.

One private lottery of the day deserves mention. In 1826, Thomas Jefferson, eighty-three, in the last year of his life and heavily burdened with debts, wrote to James Madison, explaining that because of his sad financial plight, combined with the low prevailing prices for land, he had decided to attempt to dispose of the bulk of his holdings by means of a lottery. Jefferson made an impassioned appeal to the Virginia state legislature, one that could not help but sadden his friends. In part, Jefferson said:

> . . . My request is, only to be permitted to sell my own property freely to pay my own debts . . . To sell it in a way which will offend no moral principle, and expose none to risk but the willing, and those wishing to be permitted to take the chance of gain. To give me, in short, that permission which you often allow to persons not more moral.
>
> Will it be objected, that although not evil in itself, it may, as a precedent lead to evil? But let those who shall quote the precedent bring their case within the same measure. Have they, as in this

35

case, devoted three-score years and one of their lives, uninterrupt-
edly to the service of their country? . . . Have the stations of their
trial been of equal importance? . . . If all these circumstances,
which characterize the present case, have taken place in theirs also,
then follow the precedent . . . It will not impoverish your treasury,
as it takes nothing from that, and asks but a simple permission, by
an act of natural right, to do one of moral justice.

Jefferson's petition was granted, but he never lived to see his
financial problems resolved. The incident remains a sad final
chapter in the great man's life.

One of the most criticized lotteries of the time was meant to
raise money to build the nation's capital city. Congress had a
location for the city, a land area ten miles square which had
been ceded from the states of Maryland and Virginia. The name
"Washington" was suggested by the Commissioners of the District of Columbia after consultation with Jefferson and Madison.
To design the city plan, the services of architect-engineer Major
Pierre-Charles L'Enfant were accepted.

All that was lacking was money. In 1793, the Commissioners,
acting "with previous approbation of the President," launched
a huge lottery of several classes. It involved the sale of 50,000
tickets—16,737 prizes, 33,263 blanks—at $7.00 each. The
grand prize was "one superb hotel, with baths, outhouses, etc.,
to cost $50,000."

Ticket sales got off to a rousing start, with chances being
marketed as far west as the Michigan Territory. But several
other lotteries were being conducted at the same time, and the
competition for customers became intense. Ticket sales slumped
sharply. Samuel Blodget, the lottery agent, and the city's construction supervisor as well, managed to begin the drawing of
the first class on the appointed date, but only because a group of
community-spirited citizens agreed to buy up all the remaining
tickets.

The drawing went slowly, with only a relatively few tickets

being pulled each day. Accusations of fraud began to be heard. One charge had it that the numbers for the larger prizes had never been put into the wheel.

Blodget paid no heed to the accusations and went ahead with the selling of tickets in the second class, even before the first-class drawings had been completed. This alarmed the Commissioners, and President Washington, too. Blodget was forced to pledge personal property and stocks guaranteeing the payment of prizes.

This did not end the matter. Indeed, conditions worsened. The grand prize winner was startled to find that the hotel he had won was still under construction. He brought a lawsuit against Blodget to collect the full value of his prize—$50,000. The litigation went on for years.

The drawing for the second-class tickets was supposed to begin in December, 1794, but so few tickets had been sold by that date that the lottery was postponed. Finally, on July 4, 1796, the drawing began. Only about a hundred chances were drawn each week. The *Washington Gazette* figured out that at that rate it would take ten years to complete the drawing. The newspaper suggested that people mention their ownership of tickets in their wills. Before the year was over, Blodget halted the drawings, and did not resume them until two-and-one-half years later. In 1799, he decided to terminate the lottery entirely.

The "Federal Lottery," as it was sometimes called, infuriated everyone—the Commissioners of the District of Columbia and Congress, not to mention the people who had purchased tickets. When, in 1805, a request for a lottery to subsidize a university as a "Permanent institution for the education of young in the City of Washington" was put before Congress, it was quickly rejected.

As the number of lotteries spiraled upward, and the sums of money involved increased in size, professional ticket sellers entered the field. At first, these brokers operated their businesses

37

Lottery handbills often featured Dame Fortune.

as mere sidelines to their regular occupations. But such was the growth of lottery activity, and so rewarding did the business become, that brokers began to devote themselves to ticket-selling exclusively. The practice became widespread in a remarkably short time. By 1815, according to *Fortune's Merry Wheel*, ". . . every town of one thousand persons or more had its middlemen whose business was any and all transactions connected with selling lottery tickets."

Throughout the early decades of the nineteenth century, the role of the broker continued to increase in importance. Besides selling tickets, brokers eventually completely controlled and supervised lotteries for the sponsoring parties.

A broker would contact an institution, perhaps a church or a college, that had previously been granted a lottery franchise. He would convince the principal authorities that by virtue of his experience and the size of his operation, he could sell a far greater number of tickets than they themselves ever could. The next step was to have the state legislature assign the franchise to the agent. The broker received either a fixed sum or a percentage of the total amount realized through ticket sales.

The lottery-brokerage firms of this period have been compared to Wall Street stock brokers of the present day. When a major American corporation seeks to raise a substantial amount of money for development work or expansion, the corporation does not go to the public directly. Instead, the corporation employs a

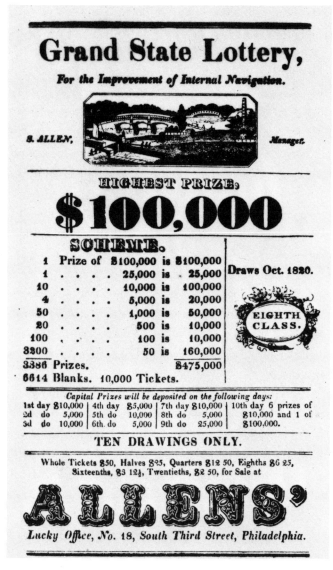

A lottery handbill of the 1820's.

broker, a firm that sells the company's stocks or bonds or both to the general public in return for a commission on the amount sold. So it was with the nineteenth-century lottery broker.

Like his twentieth-century counterpart, the lottery broker of the past century might have a number of branch offices, or he would negotiate working agreements with firms in other cities. Brokers were responsible for spreading the lottery over the face of America, into the smallest towns and villages.

In dealing with those who wished to raise money by means of lotteries, principally municipal or state governments, and handling their day-to-day affairs with their customers, lottery brokers became skilled in dealing in currency of all types, and in bank notes and promissary notes. It was thus a very short step from lottery-brokering to banking.

It is more than a coincidence that some of the country's largest banking institutions were founded by lottery brokers. The outstanding example is John Thompson, who began his career as a lottery ticket salesman. Thompson went on to found the First National Bank of New York City, which was chartered in 1863, and was one of the founders of the Chase National Bank, chartered in 1873. Known today as the Chase Manhattan Corporation, it ranks as the nation's second largest commercial banking company.

Every manner and means of sales promotion was used to stimulate ticket sales. Agents and brokers advertised in newspapers. They prepared and distributed handbills and broadsides. Jingles and songs were not uncommon.

The Independent Chronicle of Boston carried this advertisment on March 8, 1808:

20,000 DOLLARS!!!
The Great Prize of Twenty Thousand
Dollars was on last Monday drawn against
No. 21549
In Harvard College Lottery and was sold in
Quarters at Gilbert and Dean's Real Fortunate
Lottery Office No. 79 State St.
The two largest prizes ever known in the
Northern States have been sold by Gilbert
and Dean

DRAWN NUMBERS IN THE NEW-YORK STATE

LITERATURE LOTTERY,
Class No. FOUR, for 1826.

38, 57, 1, 45, 11, 26, 7, 19.

Literature Lottery,
Class Number 5, for 1826.
J. B. YATES, and A. McINTYRE, Managers.

60 NUMBERS, EIGHT BALLOTS TO BE DRAWN.

To be drawn on the 30th day of August next.

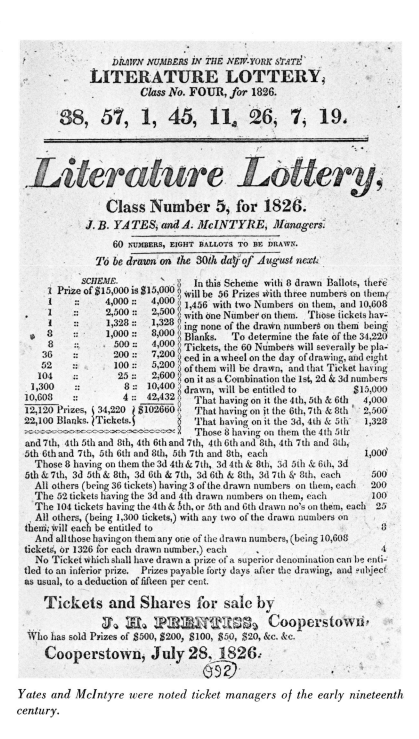

SCHEME.			
1 Prize of	$15,000	is $15,000	
1	:: 4,000	:: 4,000	
1	:: 2,500	:: 2,500	
1	:: 1,328	:: 1,328	
3	:: 1,000	:: 3,000	
8	:: 500	:: 4,000	
36	:: 200	:: 7,200	
52	:: 100	:: 5,200	
104	:: 25	:: 2,600	
1,300	:: 8	:: 10,400	
10,608	:: 4	:: 42,432	

12,120 Prizes, 34,220 $102660
22,100 Blanks. Tickets.

In this Scheme with 8 drawn Ballots, there will be 56 Prizes with three numbers on them, 1,456 with two Numbers on them, and 10,608 with one Number on them. Those tickets having none of the drawn numbers on them being Blanks. To determine the fate of the 34,220 Tickets, the 60 Numbers will severally be placed in a wheel on the day of drawing, and eight of them will be drawn, and that Ticket having on it as a Combination the 1st, 2d & 3d numbers drawn, will be entitled to $15,000

That having on it the 4th, 5th & 6th 4,000
That having on it the 6th, 7th & 8th 2,500
That having on it the 3d, 4th & 5th 1,328

Those 8 having on them the 4th 5th and 7th, 4th 5th and 8th, 4th 6th and 7th, 4th 6th and 8th, 4th 7th and 8th, 5th 6th and 7th, 5th 6th and 8th, 5th 7th and 8th, each 1,000

Those 8 having on them the 3d 4th & 7th, 3d 4th & 8th, 3d 5th & 6th, 3d 5th & 7th, 3d 5th & 8th, 3d 6th & 7th, 3d 6th & 8th, 3d 7th & 8th, each 500

All others (being 36 tickets) having 3 of the drawn numbers on them, each 200
The 52 tickets having the 3d and 4th drawn numbers on them, each 100
The 104 tickets having the 4th & 5th, or 5th and 6th drawn no's on them, each 25

All others, (being 1,300 tickets,) with any two of the drawn numbers on them, will each be entitled to 8
And all those having on them any one of the drawn numbers, (being 10,608 tickets, or 1326 for each drawn number,) each 4

No Ticket which shall have drawn a prize of a superior denomination can be entitled to an inferior prize. Prizes payable forty days after the drawing, and subject as usual, to a deduction of fifteen per cent.

Tickets and Shares for sale by
J. H. PRENTISS, Cooperstown.
Who has sold Prizes of $500, $200, $100, $50, $20, &c. &c.

Cooperstown, July 28, 1826.
(992)

Yates and McIntyre were noted ticket managers of the early nineteenth century.

Though the lotteries soon will be over, I'm
    told,
That now is the time to get pailsful of gold;
And if there is any real truth in a dream,
I myself shall come in for a share of the cream.
We hail, ere the Sun, the first breath of the
    morn,
And 'tis said " early birds get the best of the
    corn,"
Of the *Four Twenty Thousands* perhaps for-
    tune may
Have in store one for me, as they're drawn in
    One Day!

Simple jingles were often used to promote ticket sales.

Just below this, another seller placed this advertisement:

It is a circumstance truly worthy of remark, and which will be
noticed by all who court the smiles of Fortune, that nearly all the
high prizes in this Lottery were sold at Kidder's Lucky Lottery
Office, which has now gained a high rank among those styled
"fortunate."

42

Later the Messrs. Gilbert and Dean joined forces with Mr. Kidder, a merger that inspired a broadside bearing a drawing of three fishermen in a rowboat. About them several fish were pictured, each labeled with a sum of money. This bit of verse appeared beneath the drawing:

FORTUNE'S ANGLERS
(*A new lottery song to be sung to the tune of "There are Sweepers in High Life as well as in Low"*)

> In the fish pond of fortune men angle all ways,
> Some angle for titles, some angle for praise,
> Some angle for favor, some angle for wives,
> And some angle for naught all the rest of their lives.
> (*Chorus*) Ye who'd angle for wealth and would Fortune obtain,
> Get your hooks baited by Kidder, Gilbert and Dean.

With lottery broadsides being handed out on every street corner, and with daily newspapers and street placards proclaiming the opportunities for instant wealth, thousands upon thousands of new customers were drawn into the lottery web. Lotteries were big business, very big. Philadelphia, according to John Ezell, had three stores selling tickets in 1809, sixty in 1827, and over 200 in 1833. The *Commercial Advertiser*, a New York newspaper, said that 160 lottery establishments were in operation in that city in 1826. Each shop could be selling tickets for several different ventures, and some of the large lotteries had as many as a dozen different classes involving tens of thousands of tickets.

Indeed, the country was gripped in a lottery mania. But even as the craze was reaching its most frenzied heights, the death notice for the lottery was being written. The end came slowly but surely.

43

4

Decline and Fall

Visitors to the city of New Orleans in 1888 and 1889 were both shocked and fascinated by what they saw. The city had been overtaken by a lottery, its citizens glassy-eyed with gambling fever.

Booths by the hundreds had been set up, in front of bars, grocery stores, and even churches, and cries of vendors filled the air. Ticket sellers were of all ages, from children of four or five to elderly men on crutches. One salesman lured customers by having a trained parrot pluck a "lucky" ticket from a stack.

Women vendors canvassed the city's office buildings. Children spent their Sunday school coins. Beggars stopped passers-by on the street to implore "one more nickel" to complete a quarter, the minimum ticket price.

The daily public drawings attracted huge crowds. One- and two-digit numbers were spun in a wheel and several drawn out to decide the top prizes. There was also an assortment of lesser prizes for those holding combinations of the drawn numbers, known variously as "gigs," "saddles," or "day numbers."

This was the Louisiana Lottery, the wildest betting spree in the nation's history. Agents for the enterprise sold tickets in Boston, Washington, Cincinnati, Denver, and San Francisco.

A ticket for the Louisiana Lottery.

Annual gross receipts totaled $50 million, and this in a day when the country's population was about 40,000,000 and the dollar worth three or four times what it is today.

Yet the gambling activity spawned in Louisiana was not typical of what was happening in other states, where opposition to lotteries had been building for years. As lotteries had grown in number, so, too, had increased the cries of scandal and fraud.

Take the case of a lottery authorized by the state of Massachusetts in 1812 to raise $16,000 for repairs to Plymouth Beach. After nine years of drawings, the managers stated that the lottery was still not completed; more drawings would be necessary.

The state legislature organized a committee to study the conduct of the enterprise. Its investigation revealed that the manager had sold 111,800 tickets in eleven classes, and had realized $886,439. Yet the Plymouth Beach project had received only $9,876, about 1 per cent of the huge sum that had been collected.

This evidence so shocked Massachusetts that all lotteries were put under close scrutiny. Citizens of the state also began to decry the selling of lottery tickets by promoters from out of state—so-called "foreign" tickets—within Massachusetts' borders. These and other abuses caused Massachusetts to outlaw lottery activity. A bill for this purpose won passage in the state legislature in 1833. Fines were to be assessed, and in some cases jail sentences handed down, to any person who printed lottery tickets, sold them, offered them for sale, or was found with them in his possession with the intent to sell.

Meanwhile, New York State was having its problems with the Union College Lottery. Early in 1805, the legislature granted the college an authorization to raise $150,000 in a lottery of four classes. About half the money was to go for construction of new buildings. But the sale of tickets was not successful.

This was only the beginning of the travail. In an effort to give fresh impetus to the fund-raising program, the New York State legislature, in 1814, authorized a $200,000 lottery for the college, with $100,000 of the sum to go toward building construction. What little money was received in ticket sales during the first year went to pay state-appointed officials of the lottery; the college received nothing.

In 1843, the college contracted with Yates & McIntyre to handle ticket sales, but this only worsened the situation. There were charges that Yates & McIntyre were selling more chances than they had been authorized to sell. It was alleged that they had drawn 245 classes and that ticket sales had reached the $40 million mark, a fantastic amount for the time. Eventually, college officials brought a suit against Yates & McIntyre. The state legislature in New York was attempting to untangle the affair as late as 1850.

The Union College Lottery went a long way toward putting an end to lottery activity in New York. The legislature outlawed all lotteries as of December 31, 1833, and the following year a bill was passed prohibiting foreign lotteries.

Pennsylvania had been the first state to pass antilottery legislation. According to John Ezell, 176 lotteries were authorized in Pennsylvania from 1747 to 1833. More than eight million tickets were offered for sale and prizes amounting to some $50 million were offered. These statistics are more meaningful when one realizes that Pennsylvania's population in 1830 was only 1,348,000.

46

Drawing for prizes in the "Orphan and Home Lottery" at Cooper Institute, New York, in 1861.

Early antilottery activity in Pennsylvania was spearheaded by a Quaker publication, *The Friend*. It urged the formation of a society to war against lotteries and petition the legislature to abolish them.

The Friend and other institutions of the day opposing lotteries were handed gratifying evidence in the case of a lottery being conducted for the supposed benefit of the Union Canal Company. It was charged that the broker had made enormous profits by selling tickets far in excess of the number authorized, but with no increase in the size or number of the prizes being awarded.

Antilottery feeling in Pennsylvania was brought to a peak by one Job R. Tyson, a Quaker and a Philadelphia lawyer, whose essay citing the "history, extent and pernicious consequences" of lotteries was widely distributed. Tyson won additional sup-

47

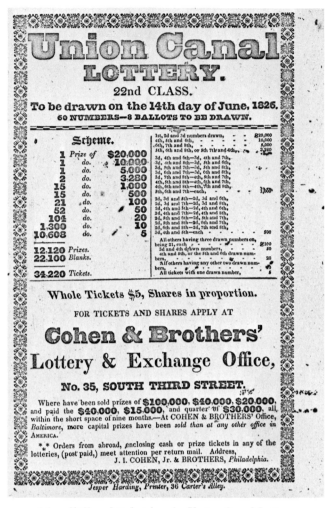

A handbill and ticket for the Union Canal Lottery.

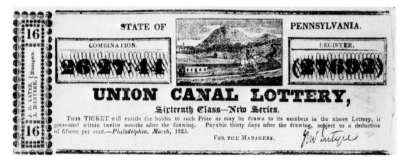

port by producing a certified list of debtors of the city of Philadelphia, which disclosed fifty-five cases of men who owed sizeable amounts to brokers for tickets. In one case the debt was $30,000.

An antilottery bill was passed by the Pennsylvania legislature early in 1833. It did not equivocate, declaring that "all and every lottery and device in the nature of lotteries shall be entirely abolished, and are declared thenceforth unauthorized and unlawful."

Ticket sellers in many states increased the wrath of reformers by promoting a subsidiary business known as "insurance," and later "policy." Meant to accommodate those who did not have the full price of a ticket, the insurance business was based on the practice of extending the drawing of tickets for each venture over several weeks, with a fixed portion drawn each day. As the drawing continued, speculation heightened as to when the undrawn numbers would be selected. So ticket sellers began to accept bets as to which numbers would be drawn the next day. Insurance "rates," or odds, were published daily in the newspapers.

A person holding a yet undrawn ticket might wager his ticket was a blank. When the ticket was ultimately drawn, and it proved to be a prize winner, the person rejoiced—naturally. But even if it were a blank, the man received something because he had taken the trouble to "insure" his investment.

Abuses of this type added fuel to the reform drive. By 1840, no less than twelve states had antilottery legislation on the books. This did not mean that all lottery activity had ceased within these states, however. Some small, private enterprises remained, but authorities considered them of no great harm.

Between 1840 and 1860, additional states outlawed lotteries, Alabama, New Jersey, and Maryland among them. Congress legislated lotteries out of existence in the District of Columbia in 1842. The antilottery feeling was so intense and so wide-

49

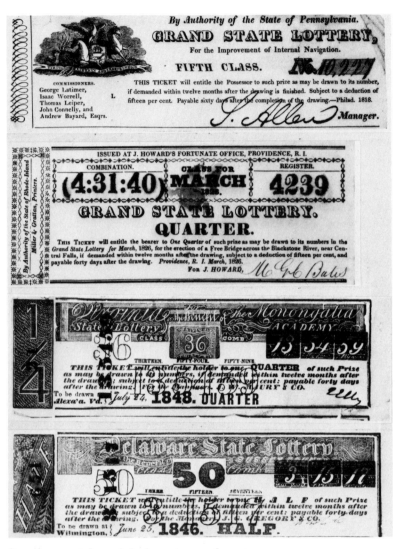

State lottery tickets of the late nineteenth century.

spread that when Texas entered the Union in 1845, its constitution contained a provision that prohibited the authorization of lotteries.

Antilottery fervor reached California with the forty-niners. At the state's constitutional convention, it was argued that since some Californians were gamblers by nature, it would be wise for the state to exercise strict control over lotteries. The final draft of the constitution banned them.

By 1862, Missouri and Kentucky were the only states that did not prohibit lotteries. Antilottery adherents could look at what they had accomplished and smile warmly. In less than half a century, the lottery had been brought from its status as a principal recreation activity, indulged in by millions of Americans, to an inconsequential street corner sport, its activity almost se-

MARYLAND LOTTERIES

FOR

FEBRUARY, 1859.

R. FRANCE & CO., Managers.

To be Drawn in Baltimore, Md., at quarter before 5 o'clock, P. M.

DATE OF THE DRAWING.	NAME AND CLASS OF THE LOTTERY.	No. Ballots in the Wheel	Number Drawn Out	Price of Whole Tickets.	CAPITAL PRIZES.	Certificate Price of Packages of Wholes.
Tuesday, February 1st	Bel Air, D	75	12	$5 00	$21,135, 2 of 5,000, 2 of 3,500	$74 00
Wednesday, " 2d	Susquehanna Canal, 1	75	12	10 00	$30,000, 20 of 5,000, 20 of 1,000, 20 of 500, 20 of 400, 20 of 250	148 00
Thursday, " 3d	Carroll County, 5	78	13	5 00	$20,000, 5 of 4,000, 5 of 2,000	74 75
Friday, " 4th	Pokomoke River, E	75	12	5 00	$24,000, 6 of 3,000, 6 of 2,000	74 00
Saturday, " 5th	Maryland State, B	78	13	10 00	$40,000, 10,000, 6,000, 3,000, 2,000, 1,592, 100 of 1,000, 20 of 400	149 50
Monday, " 7th	Washington County, F	78	14	8 00	$27,814, 2 of 5,000, 2 of 4,000	112 80
Tuesday, " 8th	Bel Air, E	75	12	5 00	$20,000, 4 of 5,000, 4 of 2,500	74 00
Wednesday, " 9th	Susquehanna Canal, 2	78	14	10 00	$31,000, 8,146, 5 of 3,500, 5 of 2,000, 10 of 1,500, 10 of 1,000	141 00
Thursday, " 10th	Carroll County, 6	78	13	5 00	$20,000, 4 of 5,000, 2,996, 20 of 1,000	74 75
Friday, " 11th	Pokomoke River, 1	78	14	5 00	$20,000, 8,000, 4,000, 1,888	70 50
Saturday, " 12th	Maryland State, C	78	13	15 00	$50,000, 15,646, 25 of 5,000, 20 of 2,000, 20 of 1,200, 20 of 1,000	224 25
Monday, " 14th	Washington County, G	75	11	8 00	$27,500, 10,648, 2 of 6,000, 2 of 4,000	125 20
Tuesday, " 15th	Bel Air, F	75	12	5 00	$20,000, 4 of 5,000, 4 of 2,149	74 00
Wednesday, " 16th	Susquehanna Canal, 3	78	12	10 00	$32,000, 10,769, 20 of 3,000, 50 of 1,000, 50 of 600	158 00
Thursday, " 17th	Carroll County, 7	78	14	5 00	$20,000, 5,608, 3,000, 2,000, 10 of 1,000	70 50
Friday, " 18th	Pokomoke River, 2	78	13	5 00	$22,988, 4 of 5,000, 5 of 1,250	74 75
Saturday, " 19th	Maryland State, D	75	12	10 00	$37,500, 20 of 3,500, 25 of 1,500, 25 of 750, 25 of 305	148 00
Monday, " 21st	Washington County, 1	78	12	8 00	$28,720, 4 of 5,000, 4 of 4,000	126 40
Tuesday, " 22d	Bel Air, G	75	12	5 00	$20,000, 10,000, 5,000, 20 of 1,000	74 00
Wednesday, " 23d	Susquehanna Canal 4	78	13	10 00	$32,500, 8 of 5,000, 4 of 2,500, 4 of 1,994, 4 of 1,500, 10 of 1,000	149 50
Thursday, " 24th	Carroll County, 8	78	12	5 00	$21,296, 30 of 1,700, 60 of 400	79 00
Friday, " 25th	Pokomoke River, 3	75	12	5 00	$20,000, 4 of 5,000, 8 of 3,000	74 00
Saturday, " 26th	Maryland State, E	78	12	20 00	$65,000, 22,680, 2 of 10,000, 20 of 5,000, 20 of 2,000, 20 of 1,800	316 00
Monday, " 28th	Maryland State, Ex. 2	...	...	10 00	$35,000, 10,000, 5,000, 2,400, 2,000, 2 of 1,000. On the Havana Plan; 20,165 prizes—40,000 Nos.	80 00
Do. "	Washington County, 2	78	12	8 00	$30,000, 12,478, 4 of 3,500	126 40

Baltimore had no dearth of drawings in 1859.

51

cret. Yet little did they realize that the lottery was to explode upon the national scene once more.

Each of three men played significant roles in the soaring success of the Louisiana Lottery. John A. Morris and Charles T. Howard, both corpulent and bearded, and bearing a slight resemblance to one another, were Northerners who had come to Louisiana in pre-Civil War days and married girls of noted families. The third man, Dr. Maximilian A. Dauphin from Alsace, a region in northeastern France, came to America at sixteen, received his medical degree in New Orleans, and continued to practice there until the lottery distracted him.

It was Morris who fathered the scheme. He had the necessary experience, training, and social contacts. His father was a well-known figure in New York racing circles, wealthy and socially active. Young Morris graduated from Harvard Scientific School and came south to marry the daughter of a well-to-do judge, one of the few men of the region who had not been ruined by the Civil War. The couple settled down on a huge estate, well-stocked with game and Thoroughbreds. Morris became well known in the business world and built the first "skyscrapers" in the South, the Hennen and Morris buildings in New Orleans, each eleven stories. Despite his prosperity and wide range of contacts, Morris could not have carried out his master plan without the aid of Charles T. Howard.

Howard's credentials were not quite so glittering as Morris'. He was born in Baltimore and came to New Orleans in 1852 at the age of twenty to become the representative for the Alabama State Lottery. After the Civil War, in 1865, Howard conducted a thriving business as the New Orleans agent for the Kentucky Lottery, operating six branch offices and rising to a position of power in the state.

When Howard and Morris joined forces, they knew exactly what they wanted—not merely the right to operate a legal lot-

"**NO SEED, NO HARVEST.**"

Safe and Sure!
Fair and Square!

THE ONE HUNDRED AND FIFTY-FOURTH

Grand Monthly Drawing

CLASS "C,"

OF THE

LOUISIANA STATE LOTTERY Co.

WILL TAKE PLACE

NEW ORLEANS, AT

Tuesday, March 13, 1883

Under the Personal Supervision and Management of

GEN. G. T. BEAUREGARD, of Louisiana,
AND
GEN. JUBAL A. EARLY, of Virginia.

IMPORTANT!

The Post-Office Department has decided that the Mails of this Company cannot be Interfered with.

We prefer that all Remittances be made by American Express Co's Money Orders. From points where they cannot be had, remit New York Exchange, Draft on New Orleans, or Post-Office Money Order. Send Currency or Coin only by Express or Registered Letter, otherwise it will not be safe.

Address, **M. A. DAUPHIN,**
New Orleans, Louisiana.

"*Safe and sure, fair and square*," declares a handbill promoting the Louisiana Lottery.

tery in Louisiana, but a monopoly franchise to do so. And that was what they were to get.

Act No. 25 of the 1868 legislature gave the "incorporators" the right to "increase the revenues of the State" through the "incorporation of the Louisiana Lottery Company." The measure exacted a $40,000 annual fee from the company, but stated that it would be exempt from all taxes. The sale of foreign tickets in Louisiana was banned.

There was considerable opposition to the granting of the franchise but it melted when the votes were cast. Years later, when the officers of the company were suing one another in a dispute over profits, it was revealed that the syndicate had boldly bribed Louisiana legislators. One man testified that Howard spent $300,000 in the first nine years of the lottery's existence for this purpose.

With expenses of this nature, it is easy to understand why the lottery was not particularly successful during the first decade of its existence. But when Morris and Howard brought Dr. Dauphin into the venture, the picture began to brighten. Dauphin hired two former Confederate generals, G. T. Beauregard and Jubal A. Early, to preside over the drawings, to give the proceedings an air of respectability and honesty. He staged them as one would a Broadway production, using the Grand Opera House and treating the public to a free concert after the winning numbers had been pulled.

As the Louisiana Lottery was developing and expanding its operations, other lotteries were collapsing. The Kentucky Lottery was held to be illegal by the Kentucky Supreme Court, and in 1878 its franchise was revoked by the state legislature. Lotteries in Georgia and Alabama were outlawed about the same time. Of course, lotteries in the northeastern corner of the United States had long since disappeared.

With its competition destroyed, the Louisiana Lottery enjoyed a period of booming growth. Tickets were hawked in almost

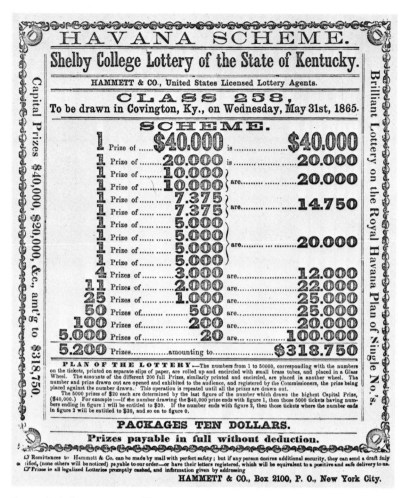

Kentucky's lottery was still going strong in 1865.

every major city of the United States.

While the financial records of the company were always secret, and its books disappeared in later years when the enterprise fell into disrepute, some idea of the enormous size of the operation can be derived from the prize lists. More than $3 million annually was distributed to ticket holders during the lottery's heyday. Reports to stockholders also give a clue to the company's success. It paid dividends of 110 per cent in 1887, 120 per cent in 1888, 170 per cent in 1889. The company's net profit during its golden years has been estimated at between $3 million and $5 million annually.

Throughout the 1880's, the Louisiana Lottery was constantly being challenged in the state legislature and the courts, yet it always managed to prevail. Countless legislators were accused of accepting bribes to vote in the company's favor, and there is no doubt that the lottery "owned" many Louisiana politicians.

Tales of men who were corrupted have endured to this day. One concerns J. Fisher Smith, a state senator of impeccable character, who, despite a condition of abject poverty, pledged he would never sell his vote to the lottery officials, no matter what they offered. But when a bill for the extension of the company's charter came before the legislature, Smith gave it his approval. Immediately afterward he collapsed and later died. A money belt containing $18,000 was found on his body.

Another legislator, the Reverend N. W. Warren, appalled the people of his district by voting in favor of lottery legislation. Pressed for an explanation, he said he did it for a cash payment that went toward putting a new roof on his church. He was banished.

Some legislators resisted the temptation, but it was not easy. One J. M. McCann of Winn, Louisiana, a stern foe of the lottery, reported finding bundles of fresh currency under his hat every time he placed it down. Money dropped from windows at his feet. Once he attended a breakfast for local politicians and discovered $20,000 in cash under his plate. McCann won legendary fame for rejecting and returning the proffered sums and for blasting the prospective donors.

Local protests against such audacity went unheard for years. Instead, Howard and his cohorts were held in high esteem. One reason was the generous donations they made toward the public good. The lottery built New Orleans' first dependable waterworks and the city's first large-scale cotton mills and sugar refineries.

When New Orleans was struck with floods in 1890, lottery funds played a significant role in relief efforts.

But while the lottery managers were able to control the situation in Louisiana, it was a different matter on the national scene, where opposition was mounting steadily. Beginning in 1878, antilottery bills had begun to be introduced in Congress, and Northern newspapers became loud in the criticism of any and all lottery activity. One of the most vocal and persistent of lottery foes was Anthony Comstock, chief agent of the New Society for the Suppression of Vice and the most noted reformer of the day. Comstock branded the Louisiana Lottery a "monstrous enterprise . . . conducted in open defiance of the law . . . demoralizing the community."

Effective opposition to the lottery also began to build within Louisiana. The Anti-Lottery League of Louisiana was founded in New Orleans in 1890, and not long after, the city of Baton Rouge played host to a convention of 956 delegates, each representing a pocket of antilottery activity in the state. For a time Morris seemed equal to the protests. He began increasing the amount the company was prepared to offer in return for renewal of its charter. He went as high as $1,250,000.

In July, 1890, President Benjamin Harrison sent a special message to Congress asking for "severe and effective" legislation which would curb lottery activity. Lotteries, the President said, "debauched and defrauded" the people of the United States. The following month Representative John A. Caldwell of Ohio introduced a bill which would deny the use of the mails to the lottery company and its agents. During debate on the measure, it was brought out that forty-two of the then forty-four states had already banned lotteries in whole or in part. No one spoke against the Caldwell bill and it passed with ease. On September 16, the measure received the approval of the Senate, and it was signed into law three days later.

This legislation proved to be a death blow for the Louisiana

Lottery. It banned all letters, postal cards, pamphlets, circulars, tickets—anything at all having to do with the lottery—from the mails. No postal notes or money orders could be issued in connection with the lottery.

According to the Postmaster General of the day, the Washington office of the Louisiana Lottery sent out 50,000 letters a month, and those received, he said, can be "safely counted by the ton." He further stated that what was true in Washington was "fivefold true of New Orleans," where an estimated 45 per cent of all post office business concerned the lottery. But with the passage of the new legislation, all such activity quickly ended. In February, 1892, the law was upheld by the Supreme Court, the court stating that Congress had the right to "designate what may be carried in the mails and what may be excluded."

The great days were over for the Louisiana Lottery. Howard had died in 1885 and Dauphin in 1890. In the face of ever-mounting hostility in Louisiana itself, the remaining officers of the company attempted to transfer operations south of the border, but they were refused licenses in Mexico, Colombia, and Nicaragua. They managed to set up shop in Honduras in 1894 and continue a haphazard existence until 1907, the year of the company's demise.

During the years the Louisiana Lottery sought to struggle on, antilottery forces in the United States continued to pressure federal legislators for additional curbs. This resulted in another bill, passed in 1895, that closed interstate commerce to lottery enterprises. It provided fines and prison terms for those who violated the statute. This law, too, was later judged valid by the Supreme Court. As the new century dawned, virtually all lottery activity in the United States had ceased.

5

By Luck of Birthday
and Other Lotteries

Not long ago Dr. Ernest van den Haag of New York University announced an idea which he felt would increase the number of people who file income tax returns. Give everyone who files an opportunity to participate in a lottery, he said. On each tax form there would be a space provided for the individual to write in a three- or four-digit number. After the tax deadline, the Internal Revenue Service would pick the winning number at random. Those who guessed right would win cash prizes.

As anyone who has filed an income tax return recently knows, Dr. van den Haag's suggestion was never adopted. The government never said why, but it couldn't have been because of a built-in abhorrence officials might have of the lottery principle. The government thinks well of lotteries, using them for a number of different reasons.

The most noted lottery conducted by the federal government is the draft lottery, known officially as the "random selection sequence system." Random selection was adapted in 1969 as part of a major revision of the draft process. The first lottery drawing under the terms of the new law was held on December 1 of that year, when 366 dates of birth were selected at random. The

Capsules are mixed before the 1969 draft lottery.

sequence in which the dates were drawn was to determine the
sequence in which draft-eligible men were to be inducted. The
first birth date drawn would be assigned random sequence number 1 and be summoned in the first draft call. The next birth
date would become random sequence number 2, and so on
through number 366.

The drawing was held in a small and crowded auditorium of

the Selective Service's national headquarters in Washington. On a table at the front of the room sat a cylindrical glass container which looked something like a water cooler. It held 366 blue capsules, each capsule containing a small piece of paper bearing a date.

Representative Alexander Pirnie of New York, ranking Republican member of the House Armed Services Committee's Special Subcommittee on the Draft, reached into the container and pulled out a capsule. In college dormitories and living rooms across the country, young men watched on television sets or listened to radios as the capsule was opened and the number read by Lt. Gen. Lewis B. Hershey, Director of Selective Service.

Congressman Alexander Pirnie draws the first capsule in the draft lottery held December 1, 1969. Lt. Gen. Lewis B. Hershey, Director of Selective Service, is at left. First date turned out to be September 14.

"September 14," said General Hershey.

Representatives of the Selective Service System's Youth Advisory Committee then drew the remaining 365 dates. As the capsules were drawn, the dates were removed and posted on a board in the order in which they had been selected.

A second drawing involving twenty-six capsules containing letters of the alphabet was also held. This lottery determined the order of call for men with the same birth date. The letter J was the first drawn, and the last was V. Thus, the first men called in 1970 were those nineteen to twenty-six years old, born on September 14, and whose last name began with the letter J.

Individuals who had priority numbers from 1 to about 120 were said to have a "good" chance of being called up for induction during 1970. For those with numbers between 120 and 240, chances were regarded as "uncertain," dependent on such things as the size of the monthly draft calls and the number of deferments granted. As for the young men with numbers from 240 to 366, their chances of being called were described as "slim." These appraisals proved fairly accurate, for the highest number called during 1970 was 195.

In the days that followed, the lottery was the number one topic among the nation's draft-eligible young men. "What's your number?" they asked one another. Some were relieved by the results of the drawing. "My future is no longer in doubt," said a twenty-year-old junior at New York University who was number 104. "I know my military commitment is more certain now."

A nineteen-old student at the state university in Portland, Oregon, had mixed emotions about the outcome of the lottery. His number was 339. "I'm lucky," he said. "But I don't know if it's that fair. I feel sorry for the other guys, the ones that are going to get called."

Of course, whether or not a young man is drafted does not depend entirely on the luck of the draw. The nation's 4,000 draft boards play a decisive role. They classify young men

A DRAFTEE'S CALENDAR FOR 1970

Under the lottery-draft, youths who are 19 through 25 years of age as of Dec. 31, 1969, and are not deferred, will be subject to call in the sequence established by the December 1 lottery in Washington, D. C. By the luck of that drawing, September 14 became No. 1 in the draft-priority list for 1970. The complete calendar for the year—

JANUARY

Birthday	Draft-Priority Number	Birthday	Draft-Priority Number
1	305	17	235
2	159	18	140
3	251	19	58
4	215	20	280
5	101	21	186
6	224	22	337
7	306	23	118
8	199	24	59
9	194	25	52
10	325	26	92
11	329	27	355
12	221	28	77
13	318	29	349
14	238	30	164
15	17	31	211
16	121		

FEBRUARY

Birthday	Draft-Priority Number	Birthday	Draft-Priority Number
1	86	16	212
2	144	17	189
3	297	18	292
4	210	19	25
5	214	20	302
6	347	21	363
7	91	22	290
8	181	23	57
9	338	24	236
10	216	25	179
11	150	26	365
12	68	27	205
13	152	28	299
14	4	29	285
15	89		

MARCH

Birthday	Draft-Priority Number	Birthday	Draft-Priority Number
1	108	17	33
2	29	18	332
3	267	19	200
4	275	20	239
5	293	21	334
6	139	22	265
7	122	23	255
8	213	24	258
9	317	25	343
10	323	26	170
11	136	27	268
12	300	28	223
13	259	29	362
14	354	30	217
15	169	31	30
16	166		

APRIL

Birthday	Draft-Priority Number	Birthday	Draft-Priority Number
1	32	16	148
2	271	17	260
3	83	18	90
4	81	19	336
5	269	20	345
6	253	21	62
7	147	22	316
8	312	23	252
9	219	24	2
10	218	25	351
11	14	26	340
12	346	27	74
13	124	28	262
14	231	29	191
15	273	30	208

MAY

Birthday	Draft-Priority Number	Birthday	Draft-Priority Number
1	330	17	112
2	298	18	278
3	40	19	75
4	276	20	183
5	364	21	250
6	155	22	326
7	35	23	319
8	321	24	31
9	197	25	361
10	65	26	357
11	37	27	296
12	133	28	308
13	295	29	226
14	178	30	103
15	130	31	313
16	55		

JUNE

Birthday	Draft-Priority Number	Birthday	Draft-Priority Number
1	249	16	274
2	228	17	73
3	301	18	341
4	20	19	104
5	28	20	360
6	110	21	60
7	85	22	247
8	366	23	109
9	335	24	358
10	206	25	137
11	134	26	22
12	272	27	64
13	69	28	222
14	356	29	353
15	180	30	209

JULY

Birthday	Draft-Priority Number	Birthday	Draft-Priority Number
1	93	17	98
2	350	18	190
3	115	19	227
4	279	20	187
5	188	21	27
6	327	22	153
7	50	23	172
8	13	24	23
9	277	25	67
10	284	26	303
11	248	27	289
12	15	28	88
13	42	29	270
14	331	30	287
15	322	31	193
16	120		

AUGUST

Birthday	Draft-Priority Number	Birthday	Draft-Priority Number
1	111	17	154
2	45	18	141
3	261	19	311
4	145	20	344
5	54	21	291
6	114	22	339
7	168	23	116
8	48	24	36
9	106	25	286
10	21	26	245
11	324	27	352
12	142	28	167
13	307	29	61
14	198	30	333
15	102	31	11
16	44		

SEPTEMBER

Birthday	Draft-Priority Number	Birthday	Draft-Priority Number
1	225	16	207
2	161	17	255
3	49	18	246
4	232	19	177
5	82	20	63
6	6	21	204
7	8	22	160
8	184	23	119
9	263	24	195
10	71	25	149
11	158	26	18
12	242	27	233
13	175	28	257
14	1	29	151
15	113	30	315

OCTOBER

Birthday	Draft-Priority Number	Birthday	Draft-Priority Number
1	359	17	288
2	125	18	5
3	244	19	241
4	202	20	192
5	24	21	243
6	87	22	117
7	234	23	201
8	283	24	196
9	342	25	176
10	220	26	7
11	237	27	264
12	72	28	94
13	138	29	229
14	294	30	38
15	171	31	79
16	254		

NOVEMBER

Birthday	Draft-Priority Number	Birthday	Draft-Priority Number
1	19	16	107
2	34	17	143
3	348	18	146
4	266	19	203
5	310	20	185
6	76	21	156
7	51	22	9
8	97	23	182
9	80	24	230
10	282	25	132
11	46	26	309
12	66	27	47
13	126	28	281
14	127	29	99
15	131	30	174

DECEMBER

Birthday	Draft-Priority Number	Birthday	Draft-Priority Number
1	129	17	304
2	328	18	128
3	157	19	240
4	165	20	135
5	56	21	70
6	10	22	53
7	12	23	162
8	105	24	95
9	43	25	84
10	41	26	173
11	39	27	78
12	314	28	123
13	163	29	16
14	26	30	3
15	320	31	100
16	96		

WHEN YOUTHS HAVE THE SAME NUMBER . . .

A local board with two or more men having the same birth date must call them in the order set by a drawing of the alphabet, which followed the birthday lottery. By the luck of that draw on December 1, men whose last names begin with "J" became No. 1, within each birth-date group. The entire sequence for 1970:

First Letter Of Last Name	A	B	C	D	E	F	G	H	I	J	K	L	M	N	O	P	Q	R	S	T	U	V	W	X	Y	Z
Priority Number	22	25	14	3	24	15	2	18	16	1	17	20	21	5	6	10	11	23	19	8	13	26	9	4	12	7

If you had been nineteen to twenty-six in 1970 and draft-eligible, would you have been drafted? Look for your birth date on this chart. Young men with draft priority numbers from 1-195 were subject to call.

(Reprinted from the December 15, 1969, issue of *U. S. News & World Report*; Copyright 1969 U. S. News & World Report, Inc.)

within their jurisdiction as "available" or "not available." They order up men for testing, rule on deferments, and grant exemptions.

The chief argument in favor of the lottery method of selection was that it would significantly reduce the period a young man would be draft-eligible. Under the former system, the period of vulnerability extended for seven years, from age nineteen to twenty-six. It was thus difficult for young men to plan their lives. Employers were reluctant to hire young men who were subject to the draft call. The lottery system changed this. If a young man gets through his year in the draft pool without being called, he can be almost certain that he will be free of any future draft threat.

The previous system was subject to many abuses and had been under attack for many years. It exempted college students. As a result more than a few young men remained in school, not so much for educational purposes, but to avoid being drafted. There were cases of youths taking "snap" courses or attending colleges where "pushover" standards prevailed. Under the lottery system, a nineteen-year-old who happens to be in college still receives a deferment, but he keeps the priority number assigned to him in the drawing. The number applies in the year his college deferment expires—by age twenty-four at the latest. The fact of his attending college has little effect on whether the young man will be ultimately drafted.

The former system was also said to be unfair in that it favored those who married young. Marriage and fatherhood were grounds for exemption. Men who did not marry were made to suffer the penalty of being draft-eligible. With the lottery system, deferment because of marriage was removed.

Draft by lottery has all the flexibility of the former method of selection. In the event of national emergency, the number of men called can be increased by simply adjusting the cutoff date.

The National Advisory Commission on Selective Service, ap-

pointed by President Lyndon Johnson in 1966, strongly recommended a random selection system. President Johnson endorsed
the method in a message to Congress in 1967. However, the
House Armed Services Committee and the military in general
were cool to the idea. It wasn't until 1968 that legislation was
passed by both Houses of Congress, clearing the way for President Nixon to issue an order creating a draft by lottery.

One criticism of the draft lottery is that it makes military
service subject to the whim of Lady Luck. Says one critic: "It
puts the solemn obligation to serve one's country on a par with
the Las Vegas gaming tables."

But in general the draft lottery has won the approval of the
press and most prospective draftees as well. One Pentagon official sums up the situation in these terms: "You can't devise
a perfect system. As long as the military doesn't need all the
young men who turn nineteen each year, some will be called and
some won't—no matter what system is used. Inequity and the
draft are just about inseparable."

The idea of using a lottery to establish those men who are to be
drafted into military service is more than a century old. It was
one of the methods of conscription used to raise Union Army
forces during the Civil War.

Through the early stages of the war, a volunteer army did
the fighting. By the middle of 1862, however, Union forces were
sorely riddled by disease and battle losses. The call went out
for an additional 300,000 volunteers in July of that year. When
volunteering proved sluggish, an Enrollment Act was passed
to provide the needed men by draft, although its actual intent
was to stimulate volunteering by threatening conscription.

The well-to-do of the day were given a means of escape. By
paying a $300 bounty, they could be excused from service or
they could hire a substitute to serve. This policy was to trigger
bloody riots.

The first men were drafted under the terms of the Enrollment

65

The Civil War draft lottery in New York.

Act in Rhode Island on July 7, 1863, and the next day in Massachusetts. On Saturday, July 11, the drawings were to begin in New York City. It was well known that there was widespread dissatisfaction in New York, but the drawings took place without any untoward incident.

The Sunday newspapers carried the names of the men who had been drafted and gave the occupation for each. It was obvious they were virtually all laboring men. Those whose names had already been drawn and those who were scheduled to be included in succeeding drawings grew angry, believing they were being forced into a war in which only poor men's blood was to be spilled.

Tension ran high at New York draft headquarters the next Monday. A revolving drum was placed on a table at the front

66

of the hot and crowded room. Small white cards, each bearing
the name of one of the eligibles and his occupation, were put in.
At ten o'clock the drawings began. A blindfolded man would
draw out a card, and hand it to the provost marshal who read the
name aloud.

So it went for almost a half an hour, with about a hundred
names being called. Then suddenly the quietness of the proceedings was shattered by a pistol shot in the street and then a
fusillade of bricks and granite paving blocks came crashing
through the windows, hurled by a mob of thousands who had
gathered outside. The wild throng attacked and took possession
of the headquarters building, driving away the provost marshal
and his deputies. They ransacked the building and set fire to it.
The blaze spread to adjacent buildings and soon two city blocks
were in flames.

Soldiers were called. They fired directly into the surging
crowd but with no apparent effect. The mob attacked, overpow-
ering the soldiers and beating several of them severely. Police
appeared to aid the soldiers. They were pelted with stones and
forced to retreat.

With these victories, the mob became more savage. They

The lottery wheel used at draft headquarters in New York, July, 1863.

67

A scene from the bloody draft riots of 1863.

stormed through the city, destroying at will. The next day was worse. The rioting masses were joined by thieves and plunderers, and widespread looting began.

Militia regiments, which had been originally ordered to Pennsylvania to resist Lee's armies, were recalled and assigned to New York. By Wednesday evening, order had been restored in most parts of the city. A notice that the draft had been suspended helped to ease tensions. An estimated one thousand deaths resulted from the violence.

68

A few weeks later the draft was resumed without incident. The practice of making a cash payment in lieu of serving was abolished in 1864, but the hiring of substitutes was permitted until the end of the war.

The Civil War draft was not successful, at least in terms of the number of men raised. Of the more than two and one-half million men who served in the Union Army, only 6 per cent were draftees. In the South, results were just as desolate. But the Enrollment Act was meant to goad men into enlisting, and in this regard it did not fail.

When war broke out in Europe in 1914, the United States had

Civil War draft cards.

only about 80,000 men in the regular army. On June 3, 1916, under mounting public pressure, Congress passed the National Defense Act, which provided for an army of 1,125,000. In line with the philosophy of President Woodrow Wilson, it was to be a volunteer army.

But the volunteers never materialized. When the United States entered the war in 1917, the armed forces totaled 378,000 officers and men. In the two weeks that followed the declaration of war, a period in which officials expected enlistments to skyrocket, only 36,000 men volunteered. Congress then passed a draft measure and the President signed it.

Officials sought to avoid the bloodshed that had marked proceedings during the Civil War by setting up civilian administration of the draft. This time there were no army officers traveling throughout the country knocking on doors, ordering young men to sign up. Local citizens supervised the selection procedures. The practice of allowing a man to pay another to serve in his place was abolished.

June 5, 1917, was named Registration Day. Men between the ages of twenty-one and thirty reported to their local draft boards to sign up. One newspaper called it a "great day of patriotic devotion and obligation." While there was something of a holiday atmosphere to the proceedings, "yet behind stood the iron hand of coercion," to quote historian Warren S. Tryon, who has noted that a few days before Registration Day, President Wilson announced that anyone who failed to report or fled to Canada faced arrest and a year in prison.

A total of 9,586,508 men registered. Since 687,000 were all that was immediately required, a lottery was held to decide which men would be called. The date of the drawing was July 20. The scene was the Senate Office Building. Secretary of War

Telegraphers transmit World War I draft lottery numbers to newspapers throughout the country.

Newton Baker reached into a big glass bowl containing 10,319 numbers in capsules, the highest number registered at any of the 4,557 local draft boards, and drew out number 258. Telegraphers flashed the number throughout the country.

The following year, age limits were extended and men between eighteen and forty-five were ordered to register. Total registration reached 24,234,021. Of this number, 2,810,296 were drafted. Draft experts have called it a "creditable performance."

World War I draft policies were closely followed in World War II, with the Selective Service and Training Act of 1940 based largely on legislation that had been enacted in 1917. Registration took place on October 16, 1940, which was several months before the United States entered the war, thus making it the first peacetime military draft in the nation's history.

Registrants, more than 16 million of them, filled out cards, giving their names, addresses, occupations, and other personal information. The local board members shuffled the cards and assigned a number to each. They were then published so that each man knew his number. Corresponding numbers were put into a bowl and a drawing was held to determine the order in which men would be called.

The date was October 29, 1940. The place was the auditorium of the War Department. For sheer drama, no lottery has ever equaled this. President Franklin D. Roosevelt, in a brief address, called it a solemn rite and said there should be "no blowing of bugles or beating of drums."

Participants in the drawing had an overwhelming sense of history. The glass bowl that contained the capsules was the same bowl used in the World War I draft lottery. The strip of yellowed linen which was used to band the eyes of Secretary of War Henry L. Stimson, who was to pick out the first number, was cut from the covering of a chair that had been used at the signing of the Declaration of Independence. And the long ladle

Secretary of War Henry Stimson prepares to draw the first capsule in the 1940 national lottery for Selective Service registrants. President Roosevelt is at left.

that was used to stir the capsules had been carved from a rafter in Philadelphia's Independence Hall.

After Secretary Stimson picked the first capsule, he handed it to President Roosevelt. The President opened it, lifted out the slip, paused, and read slowly into a forest of microphones representing all the radio networks:

"1-5-8."

Other cabinet officers then followed Secretary Stimson. Later in the day the drawing of numbers was turned over to men trained by the Selective Service Administration. Officials sought to rule out all possibility of error. Each capsule was drawn in full view of the audience and the number was announced into a microphone. Then the slip bearing the number was handed to a clerk who inserted it into a specially prepared card. Each card was passed along a row of Boy Scouts to two men who operated photographic registration devices. These camera-like machines photographed the number and the exact time each was drawn. A sequence number was also assigned to each card.

The Selective Service System of World War II has received high marks for the orderly way in which it provided military manpower. In total, more than 16 million men were called into the armed services under the provisions of the Act.

After World War I, the United States entered a period of pacifism and isolation and the draft was discontinued, but after World War II the nation shouldered a heavy burden of international commitments. As a result, President Harry Truman, in March, 1948, recommended that Congress re-establish the draft and create a program of Universal Military Training. This recommendation led to the Selective Service Act of 1948, which was to have expired in 1950. Because of the outbreak of hostilities in Korea—the Korean War—Congress extended the draft indefinitely in 1951.

Someday there may be no need for a military draft. During the early 1970's, efforts were being pressed to establish an all-volunteer army, one supplied entirely by enlistment. President Nixon favored such a course. If it should come about, the draft would be eliminated.

But many experts on the subject of military manpower believe that a volunteer army is just a dream. Curtis W. Tarr, the Director of Selective Service in 1971, often said that it would be "impossible" to recruit enough men to end the draft. If Mr. Tarr is correct, then millions of young Americans are likely to have to continue to entrust their futures to the draft lottery.

The Selective System isn't the only government agency to utilize lotteries. The Bureau of Land Management of the Department of the Interior, whose purpose it is to manage and dispose of public lands, runs a game of chance, too.

Since 1960, government land offices, almost all of which are located in the Far West, have been conducting monthly drawings for oil and gas leases. Tens of thousands of people have bought "tickets" at $10.00 each. A player "wins" when he happens to be awarded a valuable lease and a broker or oil company purchases it. Any American citizen over the age twenty-one can participate.

A Florida postal clerk won a lease for an eighty-acre tract of land in Eddy County, New Mexico. A broker for a Los Angeles oil company paid him $2,000 for it. After deducting his expenses, the postal clerk figured his profit at close to $1,900, not including a 3 per cent royalty he would receive on any oil or gas produced. A Nevada housewife, a Texas contractor, and scores of other people have been similarly rewarded.

Persons interested in a particular tract submit an application card for it. Each card must be accompanied by a $10.00 filing fee and the first year's lease payment of 50 cents an acre. If the person's card isn't drawn, the lease payment is returned.

The Wall Street Journal estimates that there are 100,000 leases on federal lands with oil and gas potential. About 1,000 of these terminate each month. As many as 30,000 application cards have been filed each month in competition for leases. The chances of winning a salable lease range from 1 in 200 to 1 in 2,500, says *The Wall Street Journal,* much better odds than those offered by state-operated lotteries.

The Department of the Interior denies it is running a lottery. It calls the procedure a "stimultaneous filing of offers to lease." It devised the drawing to replace the confusion at land offices that once characterized the competition for expired or canceled leases. More information can be obtained by writing the U. S. Department of the Interior, Bureau of Land Management, Washington, D. C. 20240.

Actually, lotteries are much more widespread than most people realize. The reason we are unaware of their prevalence is because they are not always called lotteries.

Pick up almost any national magazine and look at the advertisements. Usually there are several devoted to "sweeps" or "sweepstakes." Instead of paying a fee, the participant sends in a box top, wrapper, or label. The prizes are awarded by chance. Nothing could be more lottery-like.

Firms that sponsor such contests call them sweepstakes to circumvent state and federal antilottery legislation, most of which dates to the nineteenth century but remains in effect to this day. They also allow you to participate in these contests without actually making a purchase. These firms accept "reasonable facsimiles" instead of real box tops or labels. However, it has been established that less than 1 per cent of the entrants go to the trouble of actually copying the label or box top.

Missouri, Ohio, and Wisconsin have antilottery laws more stringent than those of most other states. Residents of these states are sometimes advised by contest sponsors to "send only your name and address on a piece of paper." The state of Washington's laws concerning lotteries are the most rigid of all. Sweeps and sweepstakes are void in that state.

The "numbers" racket, illegal by virtue of state penal codes, another type of lottery, flourishes in virtually every American city. The player bets as little as 25 cents or as much as several dollars on any three-digit number from 000 to 999. The winning number is usually derived from the last three numbers of the total amount bet at a local race track. (If the total bet were $3,474,173, the "number" for that day would be 173.) Winning betters are often paid at the rate of 600 to one, although the odds against making an accurate selection are one in 1,000.

The game of bingo, used by many churches as a fund-raising device, is based on the lottery principle. Indeed, sometimes the game is known as *lotto*. Bingo is played with cards bearing numbered squares arranged in rows. No two cards are alike. Tokens are used to cover numbered squares which correspond to numbered disks drawn by lot from a box or wheel. The player who first gets one complete row of numbered squares covered is the winner.

Perhaps the most common type of American lottery is the raffle. It is a lottery in the purest sense. A club, a church group, or any organization seeking to raise funds sells a large quantity of numbered tickets. The ticket stubs, similarly numbered, are placed in a container and the winning numbers drawn at random. Raffles, bingo games, sweepstakes, and sweeps, the "numbers" racket, the draft lottery, and the Land Bureau's "simultaneous filings"—we seem to be a nation obsessed with gambling. Yet Americans have no more preoccupation with games of chance than citizens of other countries, and compared to some of them the amount of lottery gambling we do is quite negligible.

6

Lotteries Around the World

If there is one thing that most countries of the world agree upon, it is the effectiveness of the legal lottery as a money-raising device. In nations large and small, rich and poor, developed and not so developed, people lay out their pesos, francs, shillings, kronas, rupees, yen or whatever, in exchange for the delicious dream of overnight riches. At the same time they are adding to their governments' tax revenues.

Tiny Luxembourg has a national lottery. So does France, so does Germany. England offers several different kinds. Lotteries are well known in many African nations—Nigeria, Tanzania, and Dahomey among them. They thrive in countries as different in character as Japan and Greece, or Morocco and Sweden.

The Iron Curtain is no barrier to lotteries. The Soviet Union held lotteries during World War II to stimulate the sale of Russian war bonds. With each purchase of a bond, the buyer received a lottery ticket.

Poland and Czechoslovakia offer bank depositors a savings account lottery. First prize is double the amount contained in the depositor's account, with drawings arranged so that each account in fifty wins a prize. Sometimes the prizes offered in lotteries in

A winner in France's national lottery might claim a "bouquet" with a five-million franc flower.

countries within the Soviet bloc are items which are in short supply. In a recent Bulgarian state lottery, for example, one prize was a two-room apartment in Sofia.

The International Association of State Lotteries, with headquarters in Zurich, Switzerland, has fifty-four members from forty-eight different countries. The membership list is getting longer all the time.

Canada is the latest country to display enthusiasm for the

lottery. It's not the Dominion as a whole, however, only the province of Quebec.

Montreal, Quebec's largest city—the largest in Canada, in fact—began a lottery of its own in the late 1960's, which the courts ruled illegal. But the financial success of the Montreal enterprise encouraged Quebec officials to develop a province-wide lottery. The National Assembly of Quebec gave its blessing to the idea on December 23, 1969. The first drawing was held the following March.

Actually, Quebec conducts three lotteries, not just one. There's a type for every taste and pocketbook. The "Mini-Loto," with tickets selling for 50 cents, holds drawings once a week for hundreds of prizes, including several of $5,000 each. "Inter-Loto" tickets sell for $2.00 and drawings are held once a month. The big prize is $12,500. "Super-Loto" tickets cost $4.00 and give the purchaser a chance for a top prize of $200,000. "Super-Loto" drawings are held once every three months.

Ticket sales in Quebec are handled by an army of 3,000 licensed vendors, including drug stores, tobacco shops, restaurants, grocery stores, department stores, and gas stations.

The drawing of winning tickets is a computerized affair, although a human helps. Once the computer has been put into operation, circulating ticket numbers at the rate of 90,000 per

♣ loto·québec

This modern symbol identifies Quebec's national lottery.

80

second, a guest of honor presses the "stop" button. This "freezes" the winning number.

In the case of a "Mini-Loto" drawing, a five-digit number is selected. A person with a ticket bearing all five digits wins the top prize of $5,000. But a person with a ticket bearing the last four digits gets $500, and one with the last three gets $100.

While Canada has one of the world's newest lotteries, our neighbor to the south has one of the oldest. Mexico's lottery—the National Lottery for Public Assistance, to use its official name—dates to 1770, when King Charles III of Spain established the enterprise by royal charter. Today the lottery is a highly organized operation, employing hundreds of workers in the new headquarters building in Mexico City, sustaining more than ten thousand families who make their living selling tickets, and achieving sales well above $100 million a year.

More than one and one-half million dollars is spent on lottery advertising and promotion annually. Newspaper advertisements and movie trailers heap praise upon the lottery; "Spend little; win plenty!" says a brochure that is distributed throughout the country.

Ticket selling is a national pastime. The government supervises the printing and issuing of tickets but then agents, who earn a 10 per cent commission, take over. Some agents sell directly to the general public while others have subagents to do the direct selling. Many of the subagents employ street sellers, called *ambulantes*.. They divide the tickets into minute "shares," each selling for a few pennies.

In the larger cities of Mexico, vendors are everywhere. A tourist is likely to find one walking beside him on the sidewalk when he takes a stroll, running beside his automobile as he makes his way through city traffic, or standing besides him as he eats in a restaurant.

Sometimes the sellers are very young. Sometimes they are

81

Pre-teenage youngsters conduct drawings in Mexico's national lottery.

women. Even men on crutches sell tickets.

Drawings in Mexico are conducted with elaborate ceremony, employing the services of twenty-four bellboy-uniformed youngsters in pillbox hats. They begin as lottery employees at the age of eight and must "retire" at twelve. No adult employees are allowed near the lottery paraphernalia until the winning numbers have been called and recorded.

Two boys operate an electrically-powered brass cage containing 40,000 wooden balls, one for each whole ticket in the lottery. With a noisy clatter, the balls are turned over and over, then one of the boys pulls a lever and a ball rolls from the cage into a glass bowl. Three other boys supervise a smaller hand-operated cage containing balls imprinted with the prize amounts. The rest of the boys take turns calling out the numbers.

Three drawings take place each week, with prizes ranging from $16,000 to $160,000. Three times a year there is a draw-

82

ing for the top prize. Known as El Gordo (the Fat One), it is ten million pesos, $800,000.

Puerto Rico's lottery and drawing procedures are similar to Mexico's. Street vendors do the selling, offering bundles of tickets for prospective buyers to choose from. Veteran lottery players have many ways of choosing numbers. They believe some are "beautiful" and others "ugly." But some players are philosophical. "If a person is meant to have luck, it will find him," says one. "If he's not, there's no use looking for it."

The probability of winning a prize in a Mexican or Puerto Rican lottery is much greater than in any of the state lotteries in the United States. In Puerto Rico, the ticket buyer has a 15 per cent chance of at least getting the price of his ticket back— what is known as a "refund prize." In Mexico, the percentage is as high as 31 per cent. But in United States lotteries the probability is seldom more than 1 per cent.

Lotteries prevail throughout almost all of Latin America. Argentina, Brazil, Chile, Colombia, Costa Rica, the Dominican Republic, Guatemala, Haiti, Panama are among the countries that sponsor and promote lottery activity.

The lottery is just as prevalent in Europe. England boils with lottery activity, leading all other countries.

One of England's several different types of lotteries is linked to the sale of the government's Premium Savings Bonds, which are similar to U. S. Savings Bonds. But England's savings bonds pay no interest or dividends. Instead, the purchaser is given a chance to win a prize in a monthly drawing.

The numbered bonds are sold in one-pound ($2.40 in 1972) units in several values up to £500. Each unit has a chance in the monthly drawing, with prizes ranging from £25 to £5,000. The winning numbers are selected by a computer which is known affectionately as "Ernie"—for electronic random number indicator equipment.

Each bond goes into the drawing three months after the month

ABOVE: *Located in San Juan, this is the headquarters for Puerto Rico's lottery.*

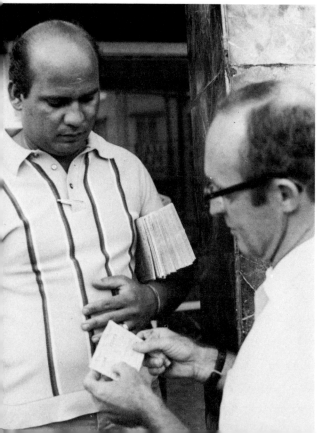

LEFT: *A ticket buyer in Puerto Rico examines his purchase. Is the ticket number "beautiful" or "ugly"?*

in which it was purchased. Thereafter it is included in every monthly drawing, whether or not it has won a prize.

The British government also controls and supervises two other types of lotteries—football pools and bingo. Football pools, the placing of bets on the outcome of big-league football (soccer) games, has the status of a major industry. About $300 million is bet each season.

For eight months of the year—August through April—more than ten million Britons are caught up in the pool mania. In clubs and pubs, on buses and trains, at dinner tables in their homes, and in the washrooms at their work, they spend their time filling out the brightly colored betting slips. Then they line up at post offices to buy postal money orders to send in with their forecasts. On Saturday, they huddle about their radios or television sets to get the results and see how they have fared.

There are a number of ways to win. From the approximately sixty major league games each week, pool promotors select what they judge to be the most difficult to forecast. A better—called a "punter"—can predict the results of fourteen different games, or pick out five teams he feels will win their "away" games, or, the most popular form, select five or more matches he thinks will end in ties.

The size of the prizes varies from week to week, depending on the number of successful forecasters. There are usually one or two punters who win $100,000 or more. The record winning amount, established in 1971, was slightly more than $1,100,000. British tax officials take a kindly view toward such windfalls and do not regard them as taxable income. Instead, the government assesses the pool operators a hefty $33\frac{1}{3}$ per cent tax on the total amount bet.

It has been estimated that approximately one-third of all betters win at least one of the smaller prizes over the course of a season, but only one in forty ends the season with a profit.

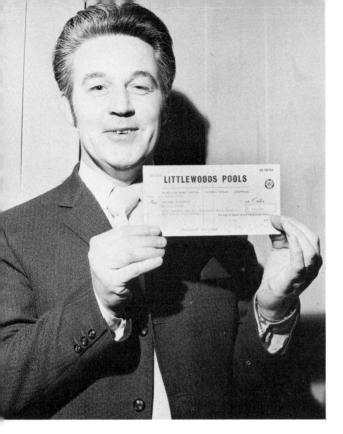

"Punter" L. Rosewood of Leeds, Yorkshire, poses with £406,761 check, a world-record prize.

While football pools are government controlled, they are operated by private companies. The two largest are Littlewoods, with about 60 per cent of the total betting, and Vernons, with 25 per cent. Both firms refer to their betting slips as "coupons," the money bet as an "investment," and any winnings that might result as "dividends."

Despite these high-sounding terms, football pool betting has all the characteristics of a simple lottery. True, there is some skill involved, and countless Britons engage in exhaustive studies of opposing teams, maintaining elaborate form books or carefully drawn charts or graphs in their efforts to boost their chances of winning. Other people follow the advice of their favorite sportswriters as set down in the daily newspapers.

But no matter how one goes about preparing himself, the odds against winning a top money prize are astronomical. Some people do their selecting by sticking a pin into the pool slip. One woman who won a big prize was asked to reveal the system she used. She said that she sat next to a window, and if a man walked down the street outside she marked the next game as a home-team win. A woman passing by indicated an away win. And a child hopping and skipping along the street meant a tie game.

To insure that no one cheats or victimizes them, pool companies maintain airtight security. At 2:30 each Saturday after-

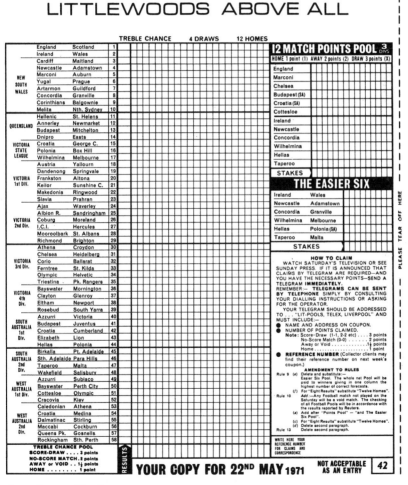

A pool entry blank or coupon.

This huge building is Littlewoods' headquarters.

noon, when the football games begin, Littlewoods, which maintains its headquarters in a stately modern building in Liverpool, cuts itself off from the outside world. The 12,000 employees who count the stake money and check the betting slips are not permitted to receive phone calls or listen to the radio. No visitors are allowed. Security men are posted everywhere.

Crooks have tried ingenious methods to communicate with cohorts inside the building. One disguised himself as a street musician and from the sidewalk outside tried to send a musical code message to an accomplice inside. The scheme failed.

Littlewoods uses the very latest electronic processing equipment. A sophisticated computer system "reads" the X's that have been entered on the pool coupons, calculates the point value of each entry, and issues a printed list of winners. Other electronic equipment keeps clients' records up to date, processing records at the rate of 900 accounts per minute.

English football pools get sharp competition from bingo. While pool revenue has fluctuated somewhat over the past decade, bingo shows consistent growth, and today plays a significant role in the social life of millions of Britons, particularly housewives.

A part of Littlewoods' computer department.

An army of clerks processes coupons.

The setting for the game is not the parish church or the county fair, which is typical of the United States. England has bingo "clubs" or "halls," more than 3,000 of them, buildings entirely given over to the game. They are likely to include restaurants or cafeterias, as well as other amenities to give an atmosphere of comfort and friendliness.

"The bingo hall is becoming the recreation center for the British housewife," says one observer. "It's a place she can go in the afternoon, meet her neighbors and friends, and enjoy herself."

More than half a million Britons patronize the bingo clubs each day. Profit is derived from an admission charge, which is usually about 50 cents. All money staked on cards is returned to the players.

These paragraphs refer only to the major types of lotteries in operation in England. In addition, there are countless smaller

Tattersall's is the most noted of Australia's lotteries.

A revolving drum and a spring-operated selection device are used in drawing winning numbers in Australia's New South Wales lottery.

drawings competing for the pocket change of the British, all permitted by Great Britain's Betting, Gaming, and Lottery Act of 1963. These include lotteries conducted by private clubs, employees' groups, or those conducted for charitable purposes.

With English lottery activity so widespread for so long—a famous English lottery to improve London's waterworks was held in 1680—it is not surprising that the British helped to establish lotteries in many other countries of the world. The United States, as previously mentioned, is one example. The British stamp is also on lotteries now active in Ceylon, Malta, and Gibraltar. Australia, too.

In 1875, one George Adams, a migrant from Hertfordshire, founded Tattersall's, Australia's most famous lottery. When the Australian government declared lotteries to be illegal and barred Adams from using the mails to promote his enterprise, he showed amazing resiliency, founding his own postal system with agents in every part of the country. Adams died a very wealthy man in 1904.

91

Buying lottery tickets in Japan.

A drawing in Tokyo.

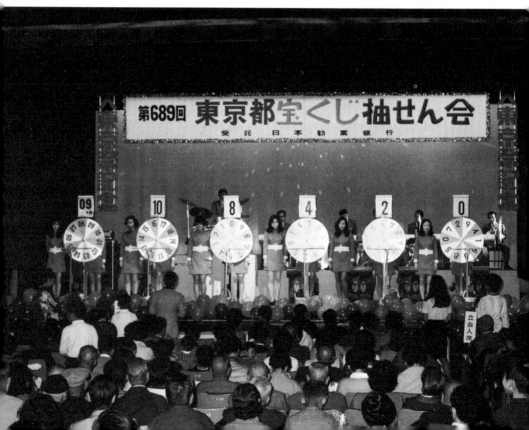

Tattersall's is a thriving operation today. In dollar volume it outdoes the various Australian state lotteries, and these account for more than $100 million in tax revenues annually.

Lotteries are also extremely popular in many Asian nations, especially Japan, where they are known as *chusen*. Japanese ticket buyers are enticed, not so much by big money prizes, but by the hope of winning goods or services that are in short supply. A prize might be admission to a select kindergarten for an infant or a scarce cemetery plot.

Because there is insufficient housing in Japan, among the most popular lotteries are those that award public housing to lucky ticket holders. In one recent year, the Japanese Housing Corporation, a semigovernmental agency, distributed more than 11,000 apartments to participants in its lotteries. Housing officials say that the lottery method of distributing apartments has its shortcomings, but they argue it is at least as good as any other system they have tried.

No discussion of lotteries would be complete without mention of the Irish Sweepstakes, which is probably the reigning king of lotteries, the biggest and best known in the world. Its roots go back more than two centuries. Since 1930, the year it took birth in its present form, the enterprise has grossed more than one and one-quarter billion dollars.

Officials of the Irish Sweepstakes state proudly that they will make payments anywhere in the world. Through 1970, they had paid winners in more than forty countries a total of over $500 million.

Irish Sweepstakes tickets cost $3.00 apiece, and the top prize is $140,000. Drawings, which are held three times a year, combine the festiveness of a county fair with the procedural elegance of a U.N. meeting. Ticket stubs corresponding to the tickets sold are mixed in a giant drum and then lottery officials pull out the winning numbers, which are then matched with the results of a horse race: the Lincolnshire Handicap run at Doncaster in Eng-

Dated 1765, this Irish lottery ticket, for the benefit of "the three United Hospitals," was a forerunner of present-day Irish Sweepstakes tickets.

land; the Cambridgeshire, also in England, at Newmarket; or the Irish Derby, at the Curragh, near Dublin. The largest prizes go to those ticket holders whose horses finish first, second, or third.

Hospitals' Trust, Ltd. is the name of the organization that operates the Irish Sweepstakes. Despite its name and its avowed purpose—to finance medical aid and hospitalization for the poor of Ireland—Hospitals' Trust, Ltd. is, according to *Fortune Magazine*, "a private company run for profit." Says *Fortune*: "It's handful of stockholders have used their earnings from the Sweepstakes to build a group of industrial enterprises that loom quite important in the modest economy of Ireland."

This is not to say that some of the money gained from ticket sales has not gone for medical assistance for Ireland's poor. Officials of Hospitals Trust, Ltd. say that the total is over $200 million. However, the Irish government says that the figure is only about 70 per cent of that amount.

What's extraordinary about the Irish Sweepstakes is that it's illegal everywhere except Ireland. Ticket sales abroad must be carried out with all the cloak-and-dagger methods of an international espionage organization. In some countries, agents are known by numbers. They communicate with Dublin through a code system. The biggest problem is the tickets. They must be brought in to the various countries illicitly, i.e., smuggled in. And the stubs must be smuggled out.

The federal government and local police in the United States have made little progress in cracking down on Irish Sweepstakes activity. Their claim is that it is difficult to obtain sufficient worthwhile evidence for a conviction.

The most notable victory achieved by U. S. law enforcement officials came in 1961 when customs agents thwarted an attempt to bring fifty cases, containing one and one-half million tickets, into the United States at Newport News, Virginia. The crates were unloaded just before daybreak from the *Irish Elm*, a freighter from Dublin, into a waiting motor launch.

How horses place in the Irish Derby helps to decide Sweepstakes winners. This is the finish of a race at the famous Curragh racecourse.

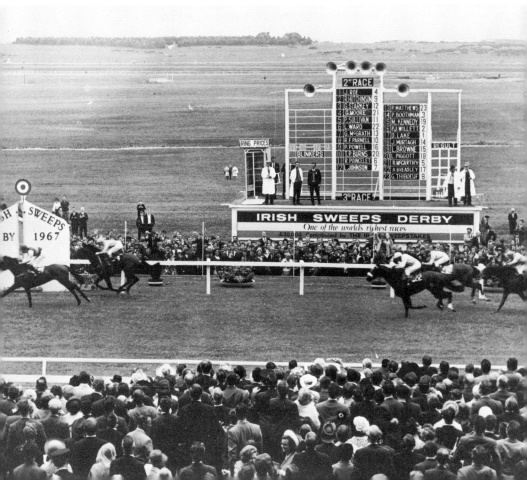

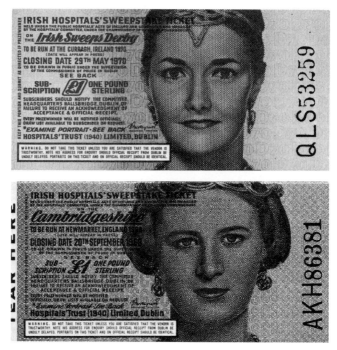

Irish Sweepstakes ticket stubs of today.

The customs men seized the launch and its two-man crew. The men were tried but the jury could not decide unanimously whether they were guilty or innocent, so they were released.

Canadian authorities have had greater success in apprehending and prosecuting Sweepstakes sales representatives. In September, 1965, state and local police in Canada launched a series of raids that resulted in the seizure of some $25 million worth of tickets, which had been shipped to Ireland from Montreal in crates labeled "table jellies." The principal distributors were arrested.

Since the Sweepstakes is an illegal gambling operation outside Ireland, the ticket buyer is at a distinct disadvantage. After he purchases his ticket, his stub is supposed to be sent to Dublin, and later he is to receive an acknowledgment of his purchase from Sweepstakes headquarters. But often no receipt is received. Either the distributor or the seller never sends in the stub (or the money), or an alert U. S. postal inspector intercepts the envelope containing the receipt.

But the buyer can't complain, at least not very loudly. After all, by virtue of his purchase, he cooperated in breaking the law.

Ticket buyers are also victimized by counterfeiters. A counterfeiter purchases a genuine ticket from Dublin, then makes a plate and prints thousands of tickets. These he sells in bulk quantities at an enormous discount to salesmen who seek out buyers.

According to *The New York Times*, Americans have been spending more than $30 million annually for Irish Sweepstakes tickets. But during the 1970's, the Sweepstakes began to encounter stiff competition as states began to legalize lotteries of their own. In time, these may accomplish what law enforcement officials and court systems have failed to accomplish.

7

Lotteries Today

During the early decades of the nineteenth century, when the public found so many lotteries to be innately dishonest, they attacked them in the state legislatures and the halls of Congress. The victory that citizens achieved was not less than overwhelming.

By 1930, every one of the forty-five states had passed statutes outlawing lotteries. State constitutions in thirty-five states prohibited all lottery activity. Countless city ordinances banned lotteries.

Federal laws prohibited the use of the mails in their connection and the promotion of lotteries as an interstate activity was against the law. In a word, lotteries were dead.

Now the pendulum is swinging back. As of 1972, three states —New Hampshire, New York, and New Jersey—were in the lottery business and several others were planning to enter it.

States have come to look upon lotteries as an efficient method of raising badly needed funds, and they have repealed or are considering repealing century-old legislation that served to ban lottery enterprises. Citizens of these states aren't objecting. They seem to favor any device that might alleviate the pressure of high taxes. Besides, there is a changing attitude toward gambling. It's not considered nearly as "evil" as it once was.

The first legal lottery drawing, aside from draft lotteries, in the United States in seventy years took place at Rockingham Park, a race track in Salem, New Hampshire, in mid-July, 1964. On a platform in front of the grandstand stood two Plexiglas drums, one large, one smaller. The smaller drum contained slips bearing the names of race horses that were entered on the special sweepstakes race to be run later in the day.

The larger drum held 333,333 lottery tickets. A handful of persons whose names would be drawn and paired with the horses stood to make small fortunes. The person who held a ticket on the winning horse would win $100,000. The second and third horses would pay $50,000 and $20,000 respectively.

A band played "The Star Spangled Banner." One by one, state officials took the microphone to salute the occasion. Governor John William King called it "a great day for our state." Three pretty and smiling young women—Miss New Hampshire and two of her handmaidens—were to do the drawing.

A flurry of excitement ran through the crowd as one of Miss New Hampshire's attendants thrust her hand into the smaller drum and drew out the name of a horse—Channan. Then Miss New Hampshire reached into the larger drum and drew out a ticket to be matched with the horse. The ticket bore the name of a Manchester, New Hampshire, overalls salesman.

The band, the pretty girls, the enthusiastic crowd—it was a gala day for staid old New Hampshire. But not everyone was celebrating. To countless New Hampshire citizens, it was a day of remorse, and they turned their backs on the speeches and the merrymaking.

The state had been divided on the matter of a lottery for years, and the issue had been the cause of much bitter feeling in the state legislature. The argument against the lottery was two-pronged. Those opposed to it declared that gambling was immoral by its very nature, and that it could not help but lead to greater corruption.

The lottery returns—Emil Simard, a member of the Governor's Council, holds aloft winning tickets following New Hampshire lottery drawing.

"House Bill 47" was the official name of the Sweepstakes Act. It called for the establishment of a three-man Sweepstakes Commission. It authorized the Commission to sell tickets at the state's three race tracks and at forty-nine state liquor stores. All profits from the undertaking were to go to the state's public school system.

In March, 1963, the Sweepstakes plan won the approval of the lower house, 196 to 166. No one was very much surprised. Similiar legislation had been introduced every year since 1953, and the house had always passed it. But just as regularly the state senate had voted down the legislation. This time, however, several senators switched sides, and the final vote was 13 to 11 in favor of the bill. One April 30, 1963, Governor King signed the measure into law.

Groups opposing the Sweepstakes had one final chance to

overthrow the effects of the legislation. The following March at New Hampshire's presidential-preference primary, voters, besides indicating which one of several presidential aspirants they liked the best, were asked this question: "Shall Sweepstakes tickets be sold in this city or town?"

Most Protestant ministers in the state urged local townspeople to vote no. "We do not believe," said the Reverend Hartley P. Grandin of the New Hampshire Council of Churches, "that the people of our God-fearing state really want this basically immoral legislation on the books." Episcopal Bishop Charles F. Hall called the Sweepstakes "this miserable intruder."

Educators, lawyers, and businessmen joined the crusade, forming an organization known as The Committee of 100. The state's newspapers and many influential out-of-state newspapers supported the Committee.

What happened was a stunning blow to the Committee. Of the 237 communities that voted on the measure, 225 voted in favor of the Sweepstakes. "There is nothing we can do now but wait and watch," said the Reverend Mr. Grandin. "Too many people in the state apparently want something for nothing."

Still, it was not clear sailing for those who backed the lottery. The federal government was preparing to harass the enterprise on several levels. Earlier, in 1963, when the Sweepstakes was being debated in the New Hampshire legislature, the Departmen of Justice had given considerable support to those who opposed the bill. A Justice Department official, in a letter to the bill's opponents, had stated that passage of the legislation would result in a "score of federal violations."

Some federal opposition stemmed from the Post Office Department. Postal authorities were wary lest New Hampshire lottery officials use the mails in conducting their Sweepstakes. Winners could not be notified by mail, nor could prize money be sent through the mails.

The Federal Communications Commission was on the alert,

too. In theory, at least, it had the right to punish any television or radio station that might broadcast lottery information, such as the names of winners.

Since it was still illegal to conduct a lottery by means of state commerce, residents of neighboring states would be violating the law if they went to New Hampshire, purchased tickets, and then brought them back across the border. The U. S. Attorney of the state of New Jersey declared that mere possession of tickets might be considered a misdemeanor, and as such punishable by up to three years in prison.

New Hampshire officials had hoped that most of the revenue to be realized from ticket sales would come from residents of states close to or bordering New Hampshire—Massachusetts, Vermont, Maine, Connecticut, and New York. Now their hopes were destroyed. How could a Bostonian, say, be permitted to buy a lottery ticket in New Hampshire and return home with it? Officials racked their brains trying to find an answer.

New Hampshire players try out state's ticket-vending machines.

They finally arrived at a clever solution. When a person makes a ticket purchase, he gives the storekeeper three dollars, and then is directed to a vending machine. The purchaser writes his name and address—or the name and address of a friend or relative—on a roll inside the machine. He then turns a crank and out comes a duplicate, while the ticket itself remains inside the machine.

The duplicate is not a ticket. It is not even a receipt. Edward J. Powers, executive director of the New Hampshire Sweepstakes Commission, calls the slip of paper an "acknowledgment." "It may seem a quibble," Powers has said, "but an acknowledgment does not constitute a claim for a prize."

Once the lottery was established as a going operation, less and less opposition was heard. New Hampshire law requires local option voting by cities and towns on the subject of the lottery every two years. In March, 1964, the vote was 3 to 1 in favor of ticket sales and 5 to 1 in November, 1966. It was over 6 to 1 in November, 1970.

While these statistics are a source of some gratification to lottery officials, the lottery has failed to live up to predictions. In one recent year, 1970, the lottery provided only $836,563, less than 1 per cent of the state's total tax revenues. Just as disappointing is the fact that receipts through the first seven years declined year by year, as this chart shows:

YEAR	GROSS REVENUE	OPERATING EXPENSES	PRIZES PAID	NET TO EDUCATION
1964	$ 5,730,093	$ 583,417	$1,799,995	$ 2,768,088
1965	3,901,596	678,192	1,400,000	2,487,365
1966	3,862,572	617,955	1,414,993	1,840,616
1967	2,567,989	577,863	943,565	1,055,199
1968	2,045,388	363,558	800,150	890,122
1969	2,001,642	358,130	790,599	868,356
1970	2,004,630	390,636	791,596	836,563
	$22,113,910	$3,569,751	$7,940,898	$10,746,309

Since 1967, New Hampshire has kept 42 per cent of the lot-

Wm S Sullivan
(NAME)

190 Pennoal St
(NUMBER AND STREET)

Springfield Mass
(CITY)   (STATE)

ZIP CODE→

STATE OF NEW HAMPSHIRE
AUGUST 6 DRAWING
1971
AUGUST 7 RACE

THIS IS ONLY AN **ACKNOWLEDGMENT** OF PURCHASE

IT NEED NOT BE RETAINED OR PRESENTED FOR PAYMENT. PRIZES
WILL BE AWARDED ON THE BASIS OF THE NAME AND ADDRESS ON
EACH WINNING SWEEPSTAKES TICKET IN POSSESSION OF
NEW HAMPSHIRE SWEEPSTAKES COMMISSION

1064607 K

NON-SALABLE   NON-TRANSFERABLE

NET PROCEEDS TO
PUBLIC EDUCATION

NEW HAMPSHIRE SWEEPSTAKES COMMISSION

Edward Powel
CHAIRMAN

Robert E Allard
COMMISSIONER

Henry P DuBois
COMMISSIONER

Edward J Powers
EXECUTIVE DIRECTOR

S-347

*Lottery tickets of the present
day from New Hampshire, New
York, and New Jersey.*

NEW JERSEY STATE   LOTTERY CO
EXECUTIVE DIRECTOR   GOVERN
50¢ New Jersey State Lottery 5

| LOTTERY | SERIAL NO. | DRAWING |
| W261 | B 308790 | 07-0 |

THIS IS YOUR LOTTERY
TICKET NUMBER   57030

NEW YORK STATE LOTTERY 11642467
DEPARTMENT OF TAXATION AND FINANCE - DIVISION OF THE LOTTERY

$100,000 First Prize
FOR EVERY MILLION TICKETS SOLD

PRINT

NAME	
ADDRESS	APT. NO.
CITY	TELEPHONE NO.

JULY 1971

$1

Norman Gallman
COMMISSIONER
OF TAXATION AND FINANCE

VALID ONLY IF DEPOSITED DURING THE MONTH OF JULY
DO NOT MAIL

NON-TRANSFERABLE   ⑈116424675 ⑈050⑈   NET PROCEEDS
FOR EDUCATION

tery income, while 18 per cent has gone for administration and promotion costs. The remaining 40 per cent has been used for prizes.

Mr. Powers says that the undertaking is hampered by federal legislation. "The full potential of this program as a revenue producer," he declares, "will not be realized until the severe federal restrictions relating to use of the mails, radio, and television are relaxed, and the same merchandising channels open to other forms of business are made available."

In New York State, where a lottery has been in operation since 1967, results have been somewhat the same. Again, officials have encountered serious stumbling blocks in the form of federal legislation.

The proposal to have a lottery in New York had to be put before the voters of the state, and they gave their approval by a margin of almost 900,000 votes. After the state legislature enacted Article 30 of the State Tax Law, the lottery was ready to begin.

The law provided that no less than 55 cents of every $1.00 in ticket sales was to be earmarked for education. Of the balance, no more than 30 cents was to go toward the payment of prizes, and the balance—15 cents—was for administrative costs, including the commissions paid vendors, salaries, advertising and promotion, ticket printing, and other expenses. (In 1970, the law was amended so as to increase the amount going into the prize fund. It was raised to 40 cents of each dollar of proceeds; the amount for education was reduced to 45 cents.)

Just as in New Hampshire, lottery advertising was not permitted on radio or television, nor could advertising or promotion material be sent through the mails or transported across the state lines. When lottery officials mapped out an advertising campaign that included outdoor billboards, they were chagrined to find that poster paper printed in New York City and intended for use on billboards in Binghamton, Elmira, and other cities

near the southern border of the state could not be shipped through either New Jersey or Pennsylvania. Trucks carrying the material had to remain within New York's borders, which meant that a more expensive routing was necessary. A matchbook manufacturer was selected for advertising on the basis that his plant was located in New York State.

It seemed for a time that New York was going to hold its lottery in utter secrecy. Not only was lottery advertising prohibited on radio and television, but lottery officials found they were to be denied use of the newspapers, too. The Post Office's ban on mailing lottery material applied to issues of newspapers that carried lottery advertising. All newspapers have some mail subscribers. Rather than disappoint these customers, newspapers rejected lottery advertisements.

A solution was furnished when one of the newspapers offered to run a lottery advertisement and then recast the page that carried the ad before the issue was mailed to susbscribers. Virtually all important daily newspapers in New York State carry lottery advertising today, but all go through the expensive replating operation, too.

The most serious difficulty New York State had to face concerned its arrangements for selling tickets. The original bill passed by the state legislature limited ticket sales to banks, hotels, motels, and branches of state and local government. By January, 1968, New York had 4,200 licensed vendors, 3,800 of them banks.

But some members of Congress didn't like the idea of banks selling lottery tickets. They felt that these institutions should not be used as a cloak of respectability for "gambling operations." In February, 1968, Congress enacted a law giving federally-insured banks in New York State one month to get out of the lottery business.

It was a staggering blow for state lottery officials. But they were successful in having the state lottery law amended so as to permit any legitimate business (except bars, grills, and liquor stores) to sell tickets. By the early 1970's, approximately 13,000 businesses were licensed as ticket vendors. About one-fourth of them were food stores. Many hundreds of drug stores, barber shops, book stores, restaurants, and gas stations were also licensed to sell tickets, and a handful of toy stores, furniture stores, and bowling alleys.

A New York State lottery ticket costs $1.00, $2.00, or $3.00. The top prize in the $1.00 drawing is $100,000. First prize in the $2.00 lottery is $25,000 a year for life, with $500,000 guaranteed. A $3.00 ticket can make the purchaser a millionaire. To lessen the tax burden, the million is made payable at the rate of $50,000 a year for twenty years. Of course, there are thousands of lesser prizes in each drawing.

When buying a ticket, a person pays the vendor and then receives a two-part ticket on which he writes his name and address. He deposits the original of the ticket in the "drop-box" provided by the vendor, retaining his copy of the ticket.

In New York State, many different types of business enterprises also sell lottery tickets.

How many tickets are winners is determined by total sales. For each one million $1.00 tickets sold, prizes are awarded as follows:

GRAND TIER WINNERS

1 at $100,000
1 at 50,000
1 at 5,000
1 at 2,000
10 at 1,000

CONSOLATION PRIZE WINNERS

300 at $500

In addition to these, there are thousands of $100 prizes awarded.

Preliminary drawings are held at lottery headquarters in Albany to determine the ticket holders who will participate in the drawing for the grand tier prizes. Each of the grand tier tickets is assigned a "post position" number.

To determine who wins which grand tier prizes, six small fish bowls, each labeled with a day of the week, Monday through Saturday, are used, plus one large bowl called a "horse bowl."

Nine sealed envelopes are placed in each of the small fish bowls. Each envelope contains a card representing a race run on a given day during a selected week at a New York race track. Volunteers from the audience then select two envelopes from each small bowl and place them in the larger bowl.

One card is then drawn from the larger bowl. This card discloses which race is to be used in determining the prizes.

The post position numbers for the horses in that race are what are significant. Remember, the tickets eligible for the grand tier drawings have previously been assigned post positions. If the winning horse in the race drawn had post position 4, all grand tier tickets which had been assigned post position 4 would win the $100,000 first prize. The post position of the horse in second place in the race determines the second-place

Players in New York check ticket post position numbers before a drawing.

winner, the $50,000 winner. The grand tier tickets with post positions for third and fourth place positions are worth $5,000 and $2,000 respectively. Tickets in the remaining post positions are worth $1,000 each.

The process sounds complicated—and it is. Why not simply issue numbered tickets with matching stubs, put all the stubs in a big drum and draw out the winners?

This reason is taxes. "A lottery of this type would subject us to federal gambling taxes," says a New York State Lottery official. "As much as 10 per cent of the total amount realized would be taken by the Internal Revenue Service. In addition, each of our vendors would have to buy a $50 federal gambling tax stamp each year. The whole thing would cripple us.

"So what we've done, and what other states are doing is basing the final results on the outcome of a horse race. Under the law, this removes our federal tax liability."

With the help of an opinion research organization, New York State Lottery officials have determined that the typical ticket buyer is a man between thirty and fifty who is married and earns between $5,000 and $9,000 a year. In buying a lottery ticket, he is motivated by the hope of winning a big prize, rather than by the idea that he is making a contribution toward his state's education facilities. Advertising messages seek to appeal to his wish. "Hit It Big!" one newspaper advertisement proclaimed. "Somebody is Always Winning; It Might as Well Be You," said another.

At first, New York lottery officials believed that the typical winner of a big prize regarded his windfall as a "dream come true." But a survey among a group of persons who had won sums of $10,000 or more, found them to have a down-to-earth attitude toward their good fortune. "We found that people who win don't fritter their money away," says one lottery official, "or at least they're not admitting it if they do."

"What have you done with the money?" was one of the questions asked in the survey. Of the 120 people queried, 47 said that they had put it into savings and investments; 17 spent some of it on travel, paid up outstanding bills, or spent it on "necessary items." Ten people bought cars. Eight paid up their mortgages or taxes. Six gave to charity; five bought new homes; two bought boats; and one said the windfall financed his campaign for political office.

How does a big winner react to the news that he is a big winner? Fifty-one said that they just couldn't believe it. "This bears out other of our findings," says an official. "When a person buys a ticket, he doesn't really think he's going to be a winner. But deep down he *hopes* he is. So he makes no plans as to what he might do with the money, and when he gets the news he's dumbfounded."

111

Lottery winners display different emotions.

Thirty-one others replied that the news they had won made them "very happy." Two were disappointed—but gave no reason.

Most winners of large sums say that the money doesn't change their lives very much. "Having it in the bank gives you a tremendous feeling of security," says one. "There's no more anxiety over money problems, no more strain. But it hasn't made much difference in our lives.

"My wife can buy more expensive cuts of meat. I can buy better suits. But I don't intend to quit my job or anything like that."

The same holds true for many others. A sixty-two-year-old Yonkers, New York, grocery store owner won $10,000 in 1967. He banked the money and continued to work from 5:00 A.M. to 9:00 P.M. six days a week in his grocery store, refusing to touch a penny of his winnings. "It will go to educate my son as a doctor," he said.

Mrs. Leon Caputo, a twenty-one-year-old Brooklyn newlywed was able to be reunited with her soldier-husband in Germany thanks to winning $100,000. A Paterson, New Jersey, man put down the name of his parish church when he bought his ticket. When the ticket won $100,000, the church used the money to build a gymnasium for its seven hundred students.

Some winners complain about the high taxes they have to pay. In some cases, the tax bite has been as much as 70 per cent of the winning sum. But most are philosophical about the problem. "It's nice to be able to afford big taxes," says one winner.

Almost all winners grumble about the crank telephone calls they receive. People demand money for causes of every type, to finance stock and real estate schemes, or to underwrite the development of inventions.

During the first four years of its operation, the New York State Lottery:

• Raised about $120 million for primary, secondary and

113

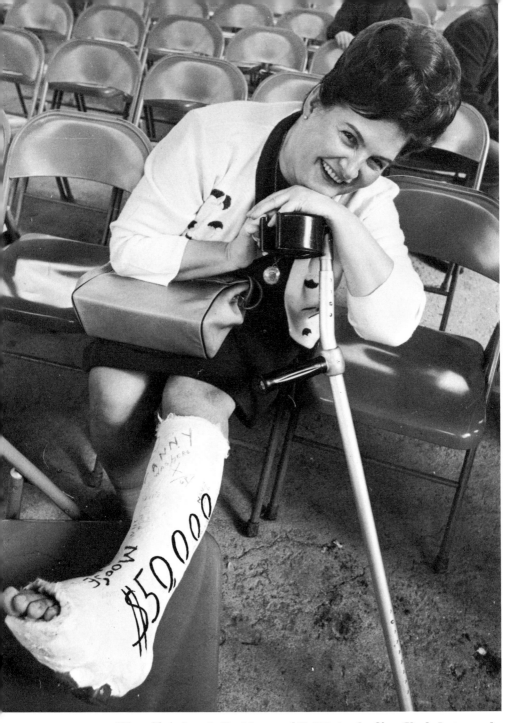

When Mrs. Joseph Tavish won $50,000 in the New York Lottery, she called it "a lucky break."

higher education, and for scholarships.

- Paid approximately $76 million in prizes to 190,000 winners, including two persons who had each won $1 million.

- Provided the state's business community with over $10 million in vendor commissions.

These statistics would seem to indicate that the New York State Lottery is a prosperous enterprise but the truth is it has not been a booming success. When the lottery was in the planning stage, it was predicted that tickets would sell at the rate of $1 million a day. Officials of the lottery now call that appraisal "fanciful" and "unrealistic." In 1970, tickets sold at about one-third of that rate.

As in New Hampshire, lottery income in New York showed an annual decline during the first years of its operation:

PERIOD	SALES	WINNERS	TOTAL PRIZES
June '67-March '68	$53,659,124	12,877	$14,765,170
April '68-March '69	$48,973,223	15,501	$13,650,050
April '69-March '70	$46,989,114	46,182	$12,761,700

In New Jersey, where the lottery made its debut in 1971, things have been rosier. During the first few months the lottery was in operation, tickets sold at three times the predicted amounts.

One reason was that New Jersey offered players better odds. Forty-five per cent of ticket sales went toward the prize fund, and 25 per cent was used for administration and promotion expenses.

Ralph Batch, executive director of the lottery in New Jersey, credits its popularity to several things: frequent drawings, inexpensive tickets, big prizes, and no fuss over filling out forms.

A New Jersey lottery ticket costs only 50 cents. They are sold at over 3,000 outlets, including newsstands, gasoline stations, supermarkets, drugstores, department stores, taverns, and restaurants. Eventually the number of vendors is expected to exceed 10,000.

115

A four-leaf clover is the symbol for the New Jersey State Lottery.

The New Jersey ticket, about the size of a business card, can be purchased as easily as one buys a newspaper. The buyer doesn't have to fill out his name and address. Each ticket is identified by a six-digit number.

Lottery drawings, held weekly, are jovial affairs, each staged in a manner similar to an audience participation television show. They include flashing lights, bouncing balls, ringing bells, a blinking computer, and a jubilant recorded rendition of "I'm Looking Over a Four-leaf Clover." Jack Taylor, who emcees the extravaganzas, has described his audience as "religiously devoted." The paraphernalia also includes a barrel of envelopes containing the results of previously run horse races. One is plucked from the barrel and used in determining the ultimate winners.

A person with a ticket whose six digits match the selected number wins $50,000. If the last five match, he receives $4,000. The last four bring $400, and the last three $40. There are 1,000 winners for every million tickets sold.

A person holding a ticket with the last two digits of the drawn number wins automatic participation in the state's "Millionaire Lottery." There are 9,000 qualifiers for every million tickets sold. The winner receives his million dollars in $50,000 installments over twenty years.

New Jersey officials are pleased with results. Receipts have exceeded original estimates by almost 100 per cent.

New York officials, after observing this success, announced changes in their lottery beginning in 1972. The price for $1.00 tickets was cut to 50 cents and the drawings were held on a weekly basis—just as in New Jersey.

New York's fifty-cent ticket bears a six-digit number, eliminating the need for filling out one's name and address. Officials rely on the number in awarding prizes. New York will retain

A prize drawing in New Jersey.

New Jersey, like New Hampshire, sells lottery tickets by vending machine.

name-and-address tickets for its $2.00 and $3.00 lotteries.

Within just a few years, lotteries have become widely known again on the American scene. They have brought sudden riches to many thousands of people and added tens of millions of dollars to state tax coffers. They have not solved the financial problems that states face nor have they been the salvation of the taxpayer. But they were never supposed to.

8

For and Against

THE COMMONWEALTH OF MASSACHUSETTS
House of Representatives, May 18, 1971
An Act Relative to the Establishment and Operation
of a State Lottery

Whereas, The deferred operation of this Act would tend to defeat its purpose, which in part is to provide at once additional revenue for the Commonwealth, therefore it is hereby declared to be an emergency law, necessary for the immediate preservation of the public convenience, and it shall take effect upon its passage.

1. This act shall be known and may be cited as the "State Lottery Law."

2. There is hereby established in the Office of the Treasurer, a Division of the State Lottery, which shall include a State Lottery Commission and a Director.

3. The commission shall have the power, and it shall be its duty, but shall not be limited to, the following:

 —The type of lottery to be conducted.
 —The price, or prices, of tickets.
 —The number and sizes of the prizes.
 —The manner of selecting the winning tickets.
 —The manner of payment of the prizes.
 —The frequency of drawings.

House Bill No. 5600, quoted in part above, was passed by the Massachusetts House of Representatives in mid-July, 1971. It is typical of legislation that has been introduced in more than a dozen states.

Connecticut, in 1971, approved a state-operated lottery. About the same time Virginia eliminated its constitutional prohibition against lotteries. Arkansas, California, Colorado, Delaware, Florida, and Pennsylvania are considering establishing lotteries.

As the subject of lotteries is debated, legislators never fail to consider the matter of control. When New Hampshire sought to enter the lottery business in 1963, state officials encountered stiff opposition on this basis. Methodist Bishop James K. Mathews of Boston, speaking at the church's annual New Hampshire convention in 1963, stated: "Again and again since colonial days, public lotteries have been resorted to for public revenue. Abuses have always followed, dishonesty and corruption have always been more prevalent. Lotteries have been difficult to control . . . and their chief fruits have been social evils and resulting frauds."

The Christian Century declared that "The bishop spoke with too much restraint. In this century," said the publication, "lotteries have been *impossible* to control."

SPRINGFIELD UNION

SPRINGFIELD, MASSACHUSETTS, TUESDAY MORNING, JULY 20, 1971   38 PAGES

Lottery Bill Rammed Through House 167-64

Measure Assailed By GOP

By PHILIP D. BRUNELLE
State House Reporter

BOSTON — The overwhelmingly Democratic House, after hours of debate and parliamentary

One after another, state legislatures are passing bills to establish legal lotteries.

120

Soaked and mutilated New York lottery tickets are dried before sorting.

Aware of this criticism, and with full knowledge of lottery history, officials in the first states to establish lotteries in recent times—New Hampshire, New York, and New Jersey—set rigorous control procedures. The best evidence of this is what happened one December afternoon in 1968 in New York City.

Just as sold lottery tickets that had been picked up from vendors were being transferred from a parked truck to the computer processing center, a violent snow squall struck. The raging wind mauled the tickets, scattering them over much of Lower Manhattan. Tickets were carried into gutters and down storm sewers. They were blown atop tall buildings and out into the

East River. Some were plastered onto sidewalks or against light poles.

The next morning the front page of a New York newspaper carried a picture of the chaos. It bore a caption that read, "How many tickets were lost?"

By the time the story had appeared, lottery officials had already organized and launched a massive task force. Its mission: to check out every ticket sold during the month of November and find out which ones were missing. Manpower and computer equipment were put to work on an around-the-clock basis.

Within minutes after the storm had wreaked its violence, squads of workers were prowling rain-wettened streets in search of tickets. Those recovered were dried and sorted.

"While we were able to assume that most of the tickets involved were bought from and deposited with vendors in Lower Manhattan, it was not safe to assume all were," one official pointed out. "A visitor from Buffalo, for example, might have purchased a ticket in Buffalo, and then deposited it in a box in Lower Manhattan. In other words, we had to check through every single ticket of the millions involved and determine which were sold, unsold, deposited, and lost."

Despite the complexity of the job, it took only two days to determine that 50,003 tickets were missing or so badly mutilated they had to be replaced. Substitute tickets were issued for all of these. In the drawing held later that month, eleven of the 50,003 replacement tickets won prizes.

So thorough was the detective work that some ticket purchasers got a "free ride" in the drawing. It always happens that some buyers forget to deposit their tickets in the vendor's box in time for the monthly drawing, but even these people had replacement tickets issued for them.

This incident is retold as an example of how lotteries are conducted today. They are characterized by the strictest accounting procedures and the tightest security precautions. It is

122

also significant that the directors of the lotteries in New Hampshire, New York, and New Jersey are all former agents of the Federal Bureau of Investigation. As of 1971, there had not been a hint of scandal or corruption associated with any modern lottery—and it is no wonder.

Another argument against lotteries is that the odds they offer are weighted heavily against the ticket buyer. This argument is not so easy to answer.

Administrative costs and operation expenses are so high that the states must keep a fat percentage of the "pool," the money derived from ticket sales. The states of New Hampshire and New York keep a whopping 60 per cent of the net proceeds; only 40 per cent goes into the prize fund. At most race tracks, almost 85 per cent of the money that goes through the betting windows is returned to the bettors. Not only are the lottery odds heavily weighted in favor of the operators, but there is the additional factor of the income tax winning players must pay.

The Treasury Department has examined the subject of lotteries to determine if such a revenue-raising system might be feasible on a national basis. But Treasury officials have decided that a national lottery "would barely pay its way." Says a Treasury spokesman: "It has been estimated that 80 per cent of lottery receipts would be used up in prize money and administrative costs." For this reason, and also because of the lack of substantial public support, the Treasury Department has not recommended a lottery to the federal government.

Those who oppose lotteries say that state governments that support them are simply unwilling to face the financial realities of the day. Honest, straightforward tax programs are the means of providing for citizens' needs. Lotteries, it is said, are an attempt by those holding political power to sidestep their responsibilities. In a message to the members of his Long Island diocese, delivered not long after the New York lottery was established, Episcopal Bishop Jonathan G. Sherman declared the

123

IN HOUSE

REGULAR SESSION, 1970

HOUSE BILL NO. 742

THURSDAY, MARCH 12, 1970

Mr. Robert F. Hughes introduced the following bill, which originated in the House, was ordered to be printed.

AN ACT proposing an amendment to the Constitution of the Commonwealth of Kentucky by repealing and striking therefrom Section 226 which forbids lotteries and gift enterprises.

Be it enacted by the General Assembly of the Commonwealth of Kentucky:

1   **Section 1.** The Constitution of the Commonwealth of Ken-

2   tucky is amended by repealing and striking therefrom Section

3   226 which reads as follows:

4   "Lotteries and gift enterprises are forbidden, and no

5   privileges shall be granted for such purposes, and none

6   shall be exercised, and no schemes for similar purposes

7   shall be allowed. The General Assembly shall enforce

8   this section by proper penalties. All lottery privileges

9   or charters heretofore granted are revoked."

10   **Section 2.** This proposed amendment shall be submitted

11   to the voters of the Commonwealth for their ratification or rejec-

This bill was introduced in the Kentucky General Assembly to repeal a section of the state constitution forbidding lotteries.

lottery was "a repudiation by the electorate to support essential services through direct taxation." The *Los Angeles Times* has stated that Latin America's widespread use of the lottery "has mischievously delayed the day of effective and equitable financing."

As one form of gambling, lotteries are sometimes opposed on

moral grounds. "We oppose gambling in any form under any auspices," the Legislative Committee of the New York State Council of Churches declared in its Statement of Principle in 1953. "The alleged good which comes from money-raising activities based on petty gambling cannot possibly counteract the evil done to society as a whole. Therefore, we oppose legislation to extend, and support legislation to curtail, present gambling opportunities."

Reverend J. Elliot Ross, C.S.P., in *Christian Ethics*, echoes this argument. Says Father Ross: "Prohibition of betting by the state is amply justified, for nothing will weaken the stamina of the people more quickly and surely than the desire to get something for nothing."

However, most theologians take a milder view. As *The Oxford Dictionary of the Christian Church* points out, there is no specific Church law that prohibits gambling.

The danger lies in excess. Gambling can be a "dangerous neurosis," say Dr. Eric Bengler in his book, *The Psychology of Gambling*. "The gambler doesn't gamble because he consciously decides to gamble," say Dr. Bengler. "He is propelled by unconscious forces over which he has no control. He is an objectively sick person who is subjectively unaware that he is sick."

It's true—some people do have an overwhelming urge to gamble. Why? What do they get out of it? Most authorities say that compulsive gamblers are not motivated so much by the hope or wish of winning large sums of money, but chiefly by the excitement of gambling, the thrill of the tension.

Dostoyevski, the great Russian novelist of the nineteenth century, was afflicted by a compulsion to gamble. He wrote *The Gambler*, a classic study.

"The main point is the game itself," one of Dostoyevski's letters confesses. "On my oath, it is not greed for money, despite the fact that I need money badly."

125

Introduced by Senator Dymally

January 13, 1971

REFERRED TO COMMITTEE ON GOVERNMENTAL ORGANIZATION

An act to add Chapter 17 (commencing with Section 7280) to Division 7 of Title 1 of the Government Code, relating to a state lottery, and making an appropriation therefor.

LEGISLATIVE COUNSEL'S DIGEST

SB 91, as introduced, Dymally (G.O.). State lottery.

Adds Ch. 17 (commencing with Sec. 7280), Div. 7, Title 1, Gov.C.

Establishes state lottery, to be administered by Controller, proceeds of which are to be used in part for support of primary and secondary education in state and in part for purposes of the lottery.

To be effective only upon adoption of Senate Constitutional Amendment No. __ of 1971 Regular Session of Legislature.

Vote—⅔; Appropriation—Yes; Fiscal Committee—Yes.

The people of the State of California do enact as follows:

1   SECTION 1. Chapter 17 (commencing with Section 7280)
2   is added to Division 7 of Title 1 of the Government Code,
3   to read:
4   CHAPTER 17.   STATE LOTTERY
5
6   7280. This chapter shall be known and may be cited as
7   the "State Lottery Law."
8   7281. The purpose of the State Lottery Law is to provide
9   for the organization and administration by the State of Cali-
10 fornia of a lottery, the net proceeds of which are to be applied
11 to the support of primary and secondary education in the
12 state.
13   7282. As used in this chapter:
14   (a) "Controller" means the Controller of the State of
15 California.
16   (b) "Commission" means the State Lottery Commission,
17 and "chairman" means the Chairman of the State Lottery
18 Commission.
19   (c) "Licensee" means a person licensed to sell lottery
20 tickets pursuant to this chapter.

This bill was introduced in California to establish a lottery.

Compulsive, excessive gambling is what is immoral. The person who occasionally purchases a lottery ticket is surely not acting in an immoral manner.

Advocates of legal lotteries admit that the urge to gamble

is a powerful one, but that it is now largely being exploited by gangster elements, as in the case of the illegal "numbers" racket. The Irish Sweepstakes, which is illegal within the United States, also feeds on the Americans' gambling urge. The solution, they good. The amount of illegal gambling will then plummet.

This argument has yet to be proven. Stealing is an irresistible urge for some people. Yet simply because laws have failed to say, is to make lotteries legal and devote the profits to the public wipe out stealing, it doesn't follow that it would be proper to legalize a form of stealing for some worthwhile cause. The solution is better laws and more rigid enforcement.

Others say it could work the other way. Legal lotteries may serve to whet the public's appetite for gambling. They might broaden the gambling base. Increase the opportunity to gamble and you increase the number of gamblers.

When lotteries were pandemic during the nineteenth century, they never were considered beneficial. In May, 1880, the Supreme Court of the United States declared: "That lotteries are demoralizing in their effects, no matter how carefully regulated, cannot in the opinion of this Court be doubted. There is scarcely a State in the Union where they are tolerated, and Congress has enacted a special statute, the object of which is to close the mails against them.

"They are a species of gambling and wrong in their influences. They disturb the checks and balances of a well-ordered community.

"Society built on such a foundation would, almost of necessity, bring forth a population of speculators and gamblers, living on the expectation of what chance might award them from the accumulation of others."

A New Jersey legislator of the present day has put it more succinctly: "Lotteries are just plain bad," he said. "They're bad for the government; they're bad for the people who buy tickets. They have a detrimental effect on every level of society."

127

What's ahead? What about the future? Will lotteries become a multibillion dollar business, with the federal government and neighboring states competing with one another for our pocket money, offering ever bigger and more enticing prizes?

As the industry continues to mushroom in size, will professional promoters enter the field, claiming they can do what state governments are now doing with greater efficiency? Is a lottery scandal in the country's future?

History doesn't necessarily repeat itself.

But it provides lessons for the future.

For Additional Reading

Ashton, John. *A History of English Lotteries*. London: Leadenwall Press, 1898.

Bender, Eric. *Tickets to Fortune: The Story of Sweepstakes, Lotteries and Contests*. New York: Modern Age Books, 1938.

Current History, June, 1968. "The Civil War and Conscription," "The Draft in World War I" and "Selective Service in World War II."

Ezell, John Samuel. *Fortune's Merry Wheel: The Lottery in America*. Cambridge: Harvard University Press, 1960.

Index

131

132

133

134

ABOUT THE AUTHOR

GEORGE SULLIVAN is a free-lance writer with more than two dozen nonfiction books to his credit. Many of his titles have to do with sports, but he has written on a variety of subjects and his most recent book was *The Complete Book of Autograph Collecting*. In researching that volume he came across historic lottery tickets, ones bearing the signatures of George Washington, John Hancock, and others, and discovered that lotteries had a rich and colorful history. The result was *By Chance a Winner*.

Mr. Sullivan was born in Lowell, Massachusetts, and received a Bachelor of Science degree from Fordham University. He lives in New York City with his wife and son, Timothy.